商业蓝图

Blueprint of Business

企业家创建成功，无风险和盈利商业模式的完整指南。

The complete guide for entrepreneurs to create successful, risk-free & profitable business model.

著：黄锦祥

By Ng Chin Siang

Contents

Chapter 1 Getting to know yourself 第1章 了解自己 1
    Understand your internal motivation 了解你的自我激励 5
    Turn your passion as your business 将热忱转化为事业 8
    Develop your habit as an entrepreneur 培养你作为企业家的习惯 13
    Start small & safe 从小处开始 18

Chapter 2 Crafting strategy - Purpose of establishment 第二章 制定策略 - 创办的目的 25
    Mission and Vision 使命和愿景 26
    Key Activities 主要活动 30
    Key resources 核心资源 36
    Key partners 主要合作伙伴 40

Chapter 3 - Value Proposition 第3章 - 价值主张 44
    Modern Elements of Value Propositions 价值主张的现代要素 44
        Utility 效用 44
        The New Economy 新经济 47
        Branding using Corporate Social Responsibility (CSR) 企业社会责任 62
        Scarcity 稀缺感 64
        Cultural elements 文化元素 68
    The framework of Value Proposition 价值主张的框架 70

Chapter 4 - Customer 第四章 - 客户 75
    Customer Segmentation 客户细分 75

- Geographic segmentation 地里分化 78
- Demographic segmentation 人口统计细分 79
- Psychographic segmentation 心理细分 80
- Behavioral Segmentation 行为细分 83
- Customer Relationship 客户关系 88

Chapter 5 Channels 渠道 93
- Channel Strategy 渠道策略 94
- Direct Channel 直接渠道 96
  - Brick and click model 上下线模式 96
  - Dropship model 直运模式 98
  - Omnichannel 全方位渠道 100
- Indirect channels-Distribution Partners 间接渠道 - 分销合作伙伴 102
  - Wholesaler 批发商 105
  - Licensing 许可证贸易 107
  - Franchising 特许经营 109
  - Original equipment manufacturers (OEM)原始设备制造商 112
  - Managed service provider (MSP) 托管服务提供商 114
  - Systems integrators (SI)系统集成商 115
  - Independent software vendor (ISV) 独立软件供应商 ... 117
  - Affinity Marketing Partnership 相关营销伙伴关系 121
  - Sponsorship Marketing Partnership 赞助营销合作伙伴 123
  - Affiliate Marketing Partnership 联盟营销合作伙伴 124
- Partner Relationship Management 伙伴关系管理 126

Chapter 6- Revenues 第六章 - 收入 129
- Revenues 收入 129

Asset sale 资产销售 130

Service Revenue 服务收入 137

Subscription 签购 139

Lending 借贷 144

Renting 出租 148

Leasing 租赁 155

Broker 经纪人 160

Licensing 许可证贸易 166

Advertising 广告 171

Revenue Management 收入管理 176

Acquiring the new customer 获取新客户 179

Retaining existing customer 留住现有客户 185

Increasing the transaction value 增加交易价值 190

Optimizing prices 优化价格 198

Chapter 7- Cost 第 7 章 - 成本 203

Financial Cost 财务成本 203

Operating expenses (OPEX)营业费用（OPEX） 204

Capital Expenditures (CAPEX) 资本支出(CAPEX) 206

Economic Cost 经济成本 208

Fixed Costs 固定成本 208

Variable Costs 可变成本 210

Sunk Cost 沉没成本 212

Opportunity Cost 机会成本 213

The formula for Calculating Opportunity Cost 计算机会成本的公式 215

Economies of Scale 规模经济 221

- Economies of Scope 范围经济 225
- Cost Control & Performance Management 成本控制与绩效管理 231
  - Budgetary control 预算控制 234
  - Horizontal analysis 水平分析 236
  - Vertical analysis 垂直分析 241

Chapter 1 Getting to know yourself 第 1 章了解自己

Do you know who you are? Knowing yourself is the process of understanding yourself on the deeper level. As an adult, we act like everyone else and feeling insecure about it. It makes you think of the way of accomplishing your dream following your own destiny. Knowing yourself means to honor your values and belief, personality, moods, habits, body, and relationships with others. It means to accept your personalities such as strengths and weaknesses, passions and fears, likes and dislikes, desires and dreams. Try this link for free personality test:

你知道你是谁吗？了解自己是在更深层次上认识自己的过程。作为一个成年人，我们的行为与其他人一样，并且对此感到不安。它让你思考按照自己的命运实现梦想的方式。了解自己意味着尊重您的价值观和信仰，个性，情绪，习惯，以及与他人的关系。它意味着接受你的个性，如优点和缺点，激情和恐惧，喜欢和不喜欢，希望和梦想。试试这个链接进行免费的性格测试：

https://www.personalityperfect.com/test/free-personality-test/
http://www.humanmetrics.com/personality/career-choices

    It is necessary to take these tests as a guiding principle to make an informed decision on your career choice. Understand how you work best under different conditions. Your hopes and dreams create the pathway of your future. They help you establish the life you can be proud of living. Your dreams matter. It is worth going after it. Don't believe in anything less. Never settle for anything less.

这些测试可作为指导原则，以便对您的职业选择做出明智的决定。了解您在不同条件下的最佳工作方式。您的希望和梦想创造了您未来的道路。它们可以帮助您建立可以自豪的生活。你的梦想很重要并值得追求它。不要质疑自己的能力。永远不要满足于现状。

If you want to become an entrepreneur, ask yourself:
What is your passion?
How do you turn your passion as your career?
How much is the capital requirement?
What products or services you provide?
What is your cost?
Who is your customer?
How to serve your customer?
How to create value for your customer?
How to sustain your business?
What are the support activities needed to create value for your customer?

如果你想成为一名企业家，问问自己：你的梦想是什么？你如何将自己的梦想变成职业？资本要求多少钱？你提供哪些产品或服务？你的费用是多少？谁是你的客户？如何为客户服务？如何为您的客户创造价值？如何维持您的业务？为客户创造价值需要哪些支持活动？

And on and on until you know everything about your idea. Invest the time on your business idea, make it as your daily routine and work on it. It is the only way to realize your dream and unleash your full potential.

一直努力实现关于你一切的想法。把时间花在你的商业想法上，把它作为你的日常作息并开始工作。这是实现梦想并释放全部潜力的唯一途径。

Understand your internal motivation 了解你的自我激励

The most important thing for an entrepreneur is passion. As the life of an entrepreneur is tough, you need to work long hours and 24/7 for your own business. Finding the industry, you love is important for you to work diligently, even with no monetary reward. Passion is a form of intrinsic motivation. It is what you feel motivated to do it even with no external rewards; you enjoy the activity or take it as a chance to learn and actualize your full potential.

对企业家来说最重要的是对工作的热忱。由于企业家的生活很艰难，因此您需要长时间工作并为自己的事业全天候工作。寻找自己喜爱的行业，即使没有金钱奖励，你也依然热忱并勤奋工作。热忱是一种内在的自我激励。即使没有任何奖励，这也是你有动力去做的事情；您喜欢这项活动，或将其视为学习和充分发挥潜力的机会。

Intrinsic motivation creates positive emotion within yourself. When was the last time you did something for enjoyment? There are several activities you can do in leisure time. For instance, you may take a photo, plant a garden, play a sport, write a story, or read a book. These activities you enjoy, create positive feelings when it gives the sense of meaning in your life. It may also give you a sense of progress when you see that your effort is accomplishing something beneficial or competence when you learn something new or become more skilled.

自我激励是在自己内心创造积极情绪。你的爱就好是什么？您可以在休闲时间进行一些活动。例如，您可以拍照，种植花园，运动，写故事或阅读书籍。您喜欢的这些活动，当它赋予您生活中的意义时，会产生积极的感受。您在学习的新知识或变得更熟练时，看到您的努力有成果或变得更加有能力时，它也可以给您一种满足感。

    Consider your motivation for reading this book. If you are reading it because you want to be gain knowledge on how to be a successful entrepreneur, you are acting based on intrinsic motivation. However, if you are reading it because you want to get rich, then you're driven by extrinsic motivation. For the third scenario, some of you may be in the situation of both. Success comes a long way, if you are not getting any reward, chances of quitting halfway are high. So, make sure you are more internally driven to be an entrepreneur. In simple words, find an activity that makes you feel happy to do it and expecting nothing in return in the initial stage of the business venture.

考虑一下阅读本书的原因。如果您正在阅读它，因为您希望获得有关如何成为一名成功企业家的知识，那么您的行为基于内在的自我激励。但是，如果你因为想要致富而阅读它，那么你就会受到外在动机的驱使。对于第三种情况，你们中的一些人可能处于两种情况。成功有很长的路要走，如果你没有获得任何奖励，半途而废的机率很高。因此，请确保您发自于内心地想成为一名企业家。简单来说，找到一项让您感兴趣并投入的事业，并在初始阶段不期待任何回报。

Turn your passion as your business 将热忱转化为事业

For those of you lack of idea on what to do, try to find any activity or hobby you enjoy the most. From there, start a business related to your interest. Other than business-related knowledge, you may need to master the domain knowledge of your business. For Example, if you would like to be a professional photographer, there's more than taking photographs. You may need to know how to start your own photo studio as a business. You must master all the other activities of your studio.

对于那些对不知道自己适合做什么的人，试着找到你最喜欢的活动或爱好。从那里开始与您的兴趣相关的事业。除了与事业相关的知识，您可能需要掌握事业的领域知识。例如，如果您想成为一名专业摄影师，那么不仅仅是拍摄照片。您可能需要知道如何创建自己的照相馆作为一门生意。您必须掌握照相馆业务的所有其他活动。

Are you skilled in exposure and lighting? Do you understand the needs for various

lenses and focal length for a different shooting scene?
Are you able to find a customer that like your photography style and willing to pay for your professional service?
Have you looked what your competitors offer in the market?
Where will you operate your business?

Even though there's always room for improvement, it's important for an entrepreneur to master the core activity of a business. You must be skillful on the domain knowledge, so gain relevant training to make the product or service marketable. Build skills at no cost. Take online courses for free from top-notch universities at edX & Coursera websites. Access the content for free and pay only for the certificate. On the other hands, try free or paid courses from Udemy. You may find skill-based courses from Udemy.

即使总有改进的余地,但对于企业家来说,掌握企业的核心活动很重要。您必须熟练和掌握领域知识,因此需要获得相关培训,以使产品或服务具有市场价值。选择免费建立技能。从 edX 和 Cousera 的顶尖大学免费获取在线课程。
https://www.edx.org/
https://www.coursera.org/
https://www.udemy.com/

If you lack the skills or training, get it without cost wherever possible. Try to negotiate with education institutions or companies to train you in exchange for services rendered. Take a paid job or an internship. Look for hands-on experience from friends, family, and skilled acquaintances. If you choose the formal education, prepare around 5 to 6 figures budget. Public university costs lesser than the private one. You should maintain a consistent source of income while you're studying -if you need to go back to school for your skill development over a long period, so prepare with enough money for the living expenses too.

如果您缺乏技能或培训，尽可能免费获得培训机会。尝试与教育机构或公司谈判，以您所提供的服务换取培训机会。从事有偿工作或实习。寻找朋友，家人和熟练熟人的实践经验。如果您选择正规教育，请准备约5至6个数字预算。公立大学的费用一般低于私立大学。你应该在学习期间保持一定的收入来源 。如果你需要长时间回到学校进行技能培训，要准备足够的金钱来支付生活费用。

Once you have decided on what business will you offer, you need to treat it seriously. Even though your business is your passion, it doesn't mean it is only a weekend activity. It means being accountable for your passion and working on it daily. Instead of setting one unachievable goal, you may subdivide the big goal into smaller attainable tasks. In this way, working to achieve all the small goals help you realize your ultimate goal.

一旦你决定了你将提供什么业务，你需要认真对待它。即使您的业务是您的梦想，但这并不意味着它只是一个周末活动。要对自己的梦想赋予行动，并且每天都在努力实践它。您可以将大目标细分为较小的可实现任务，而不是设定一个无法实现的目标。通过这种方式，努力实现所有小目标可以帮助您实现最终目标。

Develop your habit as an entrepreneur 培养你作为企业家的习惯

If you are keeping your day job, decide that you will allocate your everyday schedule for the side hustle. For example, allocate time after dinner to develop your business, stick to the schedule until it becomes a part of the day after day activity. Don't make excuses during the habit formation stage. Stick to your timetable for 21 days. It helps to shape the good habit with these consistent efforts.

如果你依然有一分正职,那么你必需充分利用工作后的时间。例如,在晚餐后分配时间来发展您的业务,坚持计划,直到它成为日常活动的一部分。在习惯形成阶段不要找借口。坚持你的时间表21天。通过这些一致的努力,它有助于塑造良好的习惯。

Keep telling yourself that you will become a successful entrepreneur. Visualize yourself as a sought-after entrepreneur as if you are already one, the more you imagine yourself to be one, the faster it accepts by your subconscious mind. You will act with confidence to achieve your dream.

with the effort. As a result, it motivates you to become a successful entrepreneur.

在工作和生活之间找到平衡点很重要。要始终保持高效，坚持 50/10 规则。不停地工作 50 分钟，休息 10 分钟。它可以帮助您保持专注而不会感到疲倦。如果你实现了一些目标，给自己一些奖赏。每当你奖励自己时，你就会重申并强化自己的行为。很快地，你会无意识地将这种积极的结果与努力联系起来。因此，它激励您成为一名成功的企业家。

Keep practicing your daily routine as an entrepreneur, don't give up easily. Be flexible enough to make changes if you're facing any difficulties. Change is the only constant thing in this world. Just be bold to embrace new ideas and face challenges along the journey.

企业家必须持续努力实践目标，不要轻易放弃。如果您遇到任何困难，请保持足够的灵活性以进行改变。改变是这个世界上唯一不变的事情。只要大胆地接受新想法并面对过程中的挑战。

Start small & safe 从小处开始

It's important to keep your current job. By keeping a reliable source of income, you don't have to worry about financial obligations. Ideally, when you start a business, try to change the role gradually from an employee to a consultant or part-time worker. It takes some time before you can make a living with a business. Furthermore, by keeping the day job is a safer path than venture into your own full-time business that hasn't produced any income yet. If you plan to start a business soon, avoid signing an employment contract with a restrictive clause, that inhibits you from pursuing the second source of income. Consider going through contract details with a lawyer.

正职可维持可观的收入来源，让您不必担心财务状况。理想情况下，当您开始创业时，尝试逐渐将角色从员工更改为顾问或兼职员工。您需要一些时间才能以自己的事业谋生。当你的事业还未有固定的收入前，维持现有的生计是一个更安全的途径，而不是冒险投入你自己的全职事业。如果您计划在近期内创业，请避免签署具有限制性条款的雇佣合同，禁止您追求第二个收入来源。考虑与律师资询合同细节。

Establishing a new business often needs a large sum of money. Use the available resources as much as you can. For instance, use a personal car for the business trip, use the garage as a workshop for products. If you have a home use it as the office or rent a co-working space with small rent. It saves a lot of money on office rent and related expenses.

创业通常需要大笔资金。尽可能多使用现有的资源。例如，使用私人汽车出差，使用车库作为产品的厂房。把你的家作为办公室或租用一个共同工作空间。这样可省下办公室租金和相关费用的大量资金。

In some point in your business, you may require a substantial amount of money to run a business. When you plan to get your funding, try to get your money from a close relative and friend. Negotiate the best term like low-interest rate, and a long repayment period; specify the loan terms in writing with clause specify if the business fails, you can pay back over a longer period. Other than that, propose the profit-sharing deals with them with no monthly payback commitment, or pay only when your business generated enough cash flow.

创业期间,您可能需要大量资金来经营业务。当您需要获得资金时,尝试从近亲和朋友处获取资金。谈判最佳条例,如低利率和长期还款期;以书面形式指定贷款条款,并指明若业务失败,您可以在较长时间内还款。除此之外,建议与他们进行利润分享交易,或不需固定还款,或仅在您的业务产生足够的现金流还款。

Find the potential angel investors or venture capitalist for funding your startup. However, if you can't get any money from them, try to get on-line financing. You may advertise the startup idea online and raise fund via a cloud-sourcing site like Kickstarter.
https://www.kickstarter.com/start?ref=learn_top Pitch your project online to the public

at large, if they like your idea, they will contribute collective fund to your project.

寻找潜在的天使投资人或风险资本家为您的公司提供资金。但是，如果您无法从他们那里获得任何资金，请尝试获得在线融资。您可以在线宣传你的创业方案，并通过像Kickstarter这样的云采购网站筹集资金。https://www.kickstarter.com/start?ref=learn_top 将您的项目在线投放给公众，若他们喜欢您的想法，他们将为您的项目提供集体资金。

Settle the monthly commitment on time, pay the mortgage, student loan, car loan, credit card bill and any loan according to schedule. It is important to maintain a good personal credit score. Only apply for an additional loan when you can afford to repay. The consistent repayment history and low debt to income ratio are the main considerations for bank approving your loan. For the interest-free fund, try to make good use on the bank 0% credit transfer of your credit card balance, apply when you can pay the monthly installment.

按时摊还每月贷款，按时支付抵押贷款，学生贷款，汽车贷款，信用卡账单和任何贷款。保持良好的个人信用评分非常重要。只有在你有能力偿还时才申请额外的贷款。良好的摊还记录和低债务与收入比率是银行批准您的贷款的主要考虑因素。对于免息基金，尽量利用您的信用卡余额的银行0%信用转账，确保您有能力摊还每月分期时才申请。

For a business loan with an interest rate, take the loan only when you can repay with the consistent income. Choose non-collateral loan over the collateral loan, so you don't have to sell personal assets when you can't pay the loan. For a collateral loan, take it when you have none other credit options left and register business entity under limited liability form. A limited liability company (LLC) is a corporate structure whereby the company owner is not personally liable for the company's debts or liabilities. In simple words, the lender can claim only company assets if the company owner defaults on the loan payment.

对于有利率的商业贷款，确保您能够偿还时才去贷款。选择非抵押贷款，当您无法支付贷款时，您不必出售个人资产。如果您没有剩余其他选择，才选择抵押贷款。在有限责任形式下注册商业实体。有限责任公司（LLC）是一种公司结构，公司所有者对公司的债务不承担个人责任。简而言之，如果公司所有者违约贷款，贷款人只能索回公司资产。

Chapter 2 Crafting strategy -Purpose of establishment 第二章制定策略 – 创办的目的

As the founder of the company, an entrepreneur must be clear about the direction and roadmap of the company. The vision and mission guide every activity in the business. It is the grand strategy that defines a company. Thus, these statements should deliver a simple and concise message to everyone in the company. It should be memorable to stick on people's mind and complex enough to deliver the purpose of the establishment.

作为公司的创始人，企业家必须清楚公司的方向和战略。愿景和使命指导业务中的每项活动。这是一家公司的宏观战略。因此，愿景和使命应该向公司中的每个人传达简洁的信息。它不但只是简单易明，并且足够复杂以传达创办目的。

Mission and Vision 使命和愿景

Mission statements emphasize current business activities. It defines the role of the company plays in the marketplace. Vision statements focus a company's future endeavors, target markets, technologies, or objectives that support the mission of a company. Values are the core beliefs of an organization. It is the guiding ethical principles that dictate how people behave in achieving the business goal.

使命是当前的商业活动。它定义了公司在市场中扮演的角色。愿景陈述关注公司未来的努力，目标市场，技术或支持公司使命的目标。价值观是组织的核心信念，道德标准决定了在实现业务目标行为方式。

Example: Coca-Cola
Mission

To refresh the world
To inspire moments of optimism and happiness
To create value and make a difference.

例如：可口可乐
使命
凉爽的世界
激发乐观和幸福的时刻
创造价值并发挥作用

Vision
People: Be a great place to work where people are inspired to be the best they can be.
Portfolio: Bring to the world a portfolio of quality beverage brands that anticipate and satisfy people's desires and needs.
Partners: Nurture a winning network of customers and suppliers, together we create mutual, enduring value.

Planet: Be a responsible citizen that makes a difference by helping build and support sustainable communities.
Profit: Maximize long-term return to shareowner while being mindful of our overall responsibilities.
Productivity: Be a highly effective, lean and fast-moving organization

愿景

人：成为一个工作的好地方，让人们受到启发，成为最好的人。
产品组合：为世界带来一系列优质饮料品牌，以满足人们的需求和需求。
合作伙伴：培育一个赢得客户和供应商的网络，共同创造共同的，持久的价值。
地球：成为一个负责任的公民，通过帮助建立和支持可持续社区来发挥作用。
利润：在充分考虑我们的整体责任的同时，最大限度地提高股东的长期回报。

生产力：成为一个高效，精益和快速发展的组织

Values
Leadership: The courage to shape a better future
Collaboration: Leverage collective genius
Integrity: Be real
Accountability: If it is to be, it's up to me
Passion: Committed in heart and mind
Diversity: As inclusive as our brands
Quality: What we do, we do well

价值观

领导能力：塑造美好的未来

合作：利用集体智慧

诚信：真实

问责制：敢做敢当

热忱：全心全意投入

多样性：作为我们的品牌包容性

质量：做得最好

Key Activities 主要活动

After crafting the grand strategy, entrepreneurs should have a clear picture of the important activities of the business. To understand or define key activities, they may refer to Porter's value chain analysis. It is one of the most comprehensive frameworks that can design necessary activities for a company. For a startup, try to keep the main activities as lean as possible, the operation unit may need to handle all the important tasks as one cohesive unit. A startup should focus on primary activities to develop the core competency. At an early stage with limited resources, the founder may outsource certain secondary activities to 3rd party vendors, as the business expanding over time forms more specialized departments to serve the needs of larger business volume.

制定宏观战略后,企业家应该清楚地了解企业的主要活动 。要理解或定义关键活动,企业家可以参考Porter的价值链分析。可以为公司设计必要活动的最全面的框架之一。对于初创公司,尽量保持精简的主要活动,企业运作单位需要处理所有重要活动。初创公司应该专注于主要活动,以发展核心竞争力。在资源有限初创时期,创始人可能会将某些次要活动外包给第三方供应商,随着业务不断扩展,创始人须设立特定的部门,以满足更大业务量的需求。

Primary Activities
Primary activities are the main activities that create goods or services. It comprises:

Inbound logistics–These are the tasks related to receiving, storing, and distributing inputs within the company. Fast and frequent delivery from the supplier helps to improve the inventory turnover. Relationships with the supplier are the key factor in creating value here.

Operations– These are the intermediary units that convert the inputs (raw material, half-finished goods) into products that customers purchase. The efficient operation unit shortens the time customers receive their products.

Outbound logistics–The activities that deliver your products to the customer. These are things like the collection, storage, and distribution systems by company logistics, and they may be internal within the company or external to your customer.

Marketing and sales–These are the processes you used to convince clients to purchase from you. The quality you offer, and how well you deliver the value proposition to them, differentiate your business from the competitors.

Service–These are the after-sales activities related to maintaining the value of output to customers.

Support Activities
These are the business support units established to support the primary functions in a company.
Procurement (purchasing)– It is the support unit gets the resources for business to operate. It includes finding the supplier and negotiating for the best prices.

Human-resource management- People are a significant asset to generate growth in business. It is important to attract and retain talent with good HR practices.

Technological development- Novel products and services developed in the process of research and development, to cope with the changing needs of the market. New technologies like machine learning, artificial intelligence and automation may change the way business produces goods or services.

Infrastructure- These are company support units that help to maintain business operation. It refers to a company management, finance, accounting, and even quality control unit.

主要活动
主要活动是创造商品或服务的主要活动。它包括：
入库物流 - 这些是与在公司内接收，存储和分配输入相关的任务。供应商的快速和频繁交货有助于提高库存周转率。与供应商的关系是在这里创造价值的关键因素。

运营 - 这些是将投入（原材料，半成品）转换为客户购买的产品的中间单位。高效的操作单元缩短了客户收到产品的时间。

出站物流 - 将产品交付给客户的活动。这些是公司物流的收集，存储和分配系统，它们可能位于公司内部，也可能位于客户外部。

营销和销售 - 这些是您用来说服客户向您购买的流程。您提供的质量，以及您为他们提供价值主张的能力，使您的业务与竞争对手区分开来。 服务 - 这些是与维持客户产出价值相关的售后活动。

支持活动 这些是为支持公司的主要职能而建立的业务支持单位。

采购 - 支持单位获取业务运营资源。它包括寻找供应商并协商最优惠的价格。

人力资源管理 - 人力资源是促进业务增长的重要资产。通过良好的人力资源实践吸引和留住人才是非常重要的。

技术发展 - 在研发过程中开发的新产品和服务，以应对市场不断变化的需求。机器学习，人工智能和自动化等新技术可能会改变企业生产商品或提供服务的方式。

基础设施 - 这些是帮助维持业务运营的公司支持单位。它指的是公司管理，财务，会计，甚至质量控制单位。

Key resources 核心资源

    Physical resources are tangible assets that used to generate sales. Retailers with shop lots and goods display shelves are the superb examples. **Financial resources** are financial assets for funding like cash, loan, or raising bond and equity. **Intellectual properties** are the creation of the mind such as the brand name, logo, patent, invention. **Human resources** with different expertise and skill sets are the most important resources. Start-up has limited resources. Thus, it needs people with more broad skills to cope with multitasking environment. After identifying key activities, try to link relevant key resources to it. We will show a few examples of how to link key resources with key activity.

核心资源

　　物质资源是用于产生销售的有形资产。拥有商店和货物陈列架的零售商是极好的例子。财务资源是用于融资的金融资产，如现金，贷款或筹集债券和股权。知识产权是智慧的创造，例如品牌名称，标识，专利，发明。拥有不同专业知识和技能的人力资源是最重要的资源。初创公司资源有限。因此，需要具有更广泛技能的人才应对复杂的初创环境。确定关键活动后，尝试将相关的关键资源链接到该活动。我们将展示一些如何将关键资源与关键活动相关联的示例。

Product-driven business has products that serve a certain segment of customer. For instance, a pharmaceutical company may need to hire scientists to develop a drug. In its key activities, it may need to emphasize technological change to create the new patent drug.

产品为主的业务必须具有为特定客户群提供服务的产品。例如，制药公司可能需要聘请科学家开发药物。在其关键活动中，可能需要强调技术变革来创造新的专利药物。

Service/professional business delivering the value proposition based on its domain knowledge. For example, a software company needs programmers as its main employee. Their key activities must focus on developing a proprietary software program.

Key Activities	Key Resouces
Product Driven- Technological change Abbott- R&D for new patent drug	Human Resource: Scientists, Pharmarcist
	Intellectual property: Proprietary process, patent
	Physical resources: Laboratory & equipments
	Financial resources: Reseach grant,cash,loan,bond, equity.
Service- Technological change Amazon -Cloud service Technological change	Human Resource: IT specialist
	Intellectual property: Proprietary software, copyright, patent
	Physical resources: IT infrastructure, Server, Mainframe, PC
	Financial resources: cash,loan,bond, equity.
Infrastructure- logistics, procurement Walmart- Receive and distribution of stocks	Human Resource: Warehouse personnel, driver, cashier
	Intellectual property: Trademark, Brand logo
	Physical resources: Departmental store, Goods, Display shelf
	Financial resources: Cash,loan,bond, equity.

服务/专业业务基于其领域知识为用户提供价值。例如，一家软件公司需要程序员作为其主要员工。他们的主要活动必须专注于开发软件程序。

主要活动	核心资源
产品驱动 Abott-研究与开发新的专利药物	人力资源：科学家，药剂师 知识产权：专有流程，专利 物质资源：实验室和设备 财务资源：研究补助金，现金，贷款，债券，股权
服务 - 技术变革 亚马逊 - 云服务	人力资源：IT专家 知识产权：专有软件，版权，专利 物理资源：IT基础设施，服务器，大型机，PC 财务资源：现金，贷款，债券，股权
基础设施-物流，采购 沃尔玛 - 货物分配	人力资源：仓库人员，司机，收银员 知识产权：商标，品牌，标识 物质资源：部门商店，商品，陈列架 财务资源：现金，贷款，债券，股权

Key partners 主要合作伙伴

Business needs key partners to optimize costs, achieve economies of scale, mitigate risks and gain strategic asset and activity to complement each other limited resources. Often times, a startup may not have the resources and expertise to produce goods on its own. It may need to outsource certain activity to the supplier or service provider.

企业需要关键合作伙伴来减低成本，实现规模经济，降低风险并获得战略资源，以互补有限的资源。一般上，创业公司可能没有自己生产商品的资源和专业知识。它可能需要将某些活动外包给供应商或服务提供商。

For the supply of products, businesses cannot manufacture all goods on its own. It may need to find a supplier of the product at a lower cost to gain profit from the margin of difference. A good relationship with a supplier is important to get fast delivery, quality products and better credit term in payment.

对于产品供应，企业不能自己制造所有商品。可能需要以较低的成本找到产品供应商，以从差异利润中获利。与供应商保持良好关系非常重要以获得供应商快速交货，优质产品和更好的付款期。

For complex finished goods, even a large corporation may not have the resources to produce everything on their own. For instance, a personal computer manufacturer needs to get components from various vendors to assemble a PC. This is due to the supplier has a large demand for a product. Thus, it can achieve the scale of economies by saving fixed cost from its business units and able to offer the product at the competitive price.

对于复杂的成品，即使是大公司也可能没有资源自己生产一切。例如，个人计算机制造商需要从各个供应商处获得组件来组装制成品。这是由于供应商产品的出货量很大。因此，它可以通过从业务部门节省固定成本并能够以具有竞争力的价格提供成品。

If a business buys materials or components from a supplier, it also reduces the exposure of business risk to the unrelated business. It doesn't have to deal with price fluctuation of raw material in production. It also reduces unnecessary operation risk and other technical difficulties of the production process.

　　如果企业从供应商处购买材料或组件，这样可以降低不相关业务业务风险。企业也不必处理生产中原材料的价格波动。从中减少了不必要的操作风险和生产过程中的其他技术难题。

Chapter 3 - Value Proposition 第 3 章 - 价值主张

Modern Elements of Value Propositions 价值主张的现代要素

We need to develop a unique value proposition to sell our products in today's competitive market. Generally, we may approach from how people perceive value.

企业家需要建立一个独特的价值主张，在当今竞争激烈的市场中销售产品。一般来说，我们可能需要理解人们如何看待价值。

Utility 效用

Most people are rational in their spending. Most of us maximize utility in relation to quality of life and availability of money. That is, most of us will buy whatever we can afford to maintain our quality of life. The utility is perceived differently by the user's preference. The options that made by everyone's one of us might not be the same. It is considered rational if we can get what we like the most within our spending power. The utility can be measured in terms like productivity, price, prestige, durability, design, convenience, risk. The choices of utility must be optimized between the different criteria. For instance, premium products must have most high-end features; medium price products offer at least average or above-average features; low price products only offer basic utility features.

Price	High	Medium	Low
Productivity	High performance.	Middle performance.	Low performance.
Prestige	Premium brand.	Established brand.	No Brand/ Not emphasize on Branding.
Durability	Lost lasting, best material.	Durable, quality material.	Short live, inexpensive material.
Design	Elegant, Estatic design	Decent design	Utility design
Convenience	Easy to use	Relatively easy to use	Need some effort to use
Risk	Low defective rate	Low defective rate	High defective rate

大多数人的消费是理性的。我们大多数人在生活质量和资金的效用最大化。也就是说，大多数人都会购买消费能力以内的东西来维持生活质量。用户的偏好有所不同。每个人所做的选择可能不一样。如果能够在消费能力范围内获得最喜欢的东西，那么这被认为是理性的。可以根据生产率，价格，声望，耐久性，设计，便利性和风险来衡量效用。企业家必须在不同标准之间优化效用的选择。例如，高端产品必须具有最高端的功能，中等价格产品至少提供平均或高于平均水平的功能，低价产品只提供基本的实用功能。

价钱	高	中等	低
生产率	高性能	中间表现	性能低下
声望	高级品牌	品牌	没有品牌/不强调品牌
耐久	持久，最好的材料。	耐用，优质的材料。	短暂，廉价的材料
设计	优雅，高端设计	体面的设计	实用设计
方便	使用方便	比较容易使用	需要一些努力才能使用
风险	缺陷率低	缺陷率低	高缺陷率

The New Economy 新经济

The value proposition must be established and delivered on a new form of technology. The Internet economy will continue to evolve substantially over the next decade, with the advent of new technology and business model. New disruptive technologies such as the Internet of Things (IoT), Artificial Intelligence (AI) and Blockchain will change the economy and job opportunity in the market. Entrepreneurs need to leverage these cutting-edge technologies to survive in the era of intense competition.

企业家必须建立独特的价值主张，并以新的技术形式提供这些成品。随着新技术和商业模式的出现，未来十年互联网经济将继续大幅发展。物联网（IoT），人工智能（AI）和区块链等新的颠覆性技术将改变市场中的经济和就业机会。企业家需要利用这些尖端技术在竞争激烈的时代生存。

E-commerce 电子商务

  E-commerce is an Internet business, which involves the transfer of information on the trading of goods and services. The famous website such as BigCommerce, Wix, Volusion offer websites design service. They are among the best choices for designing an e-commerce website without an extensive programming language. They offer plans and built-in applications for customization of your business needs. Choose a plan and features that suit the business needs with minimal effort. Then, you can concentrate on marketing and sales of your website. The online marketplace such as Amazon, Alibaba, eBay, Lazada offers a ready platform with access to its large user base. Choose a category carefully so that your products serve the niche market well. These platforms normally charge a transaction fee and commission for the online sales. If you wish to avoid a lot of hassles for the inventory work, consider the drop ship model. It begins when you receive the order from the buyer and forward it to the trusted wholesaler. The wholesaler will do the delivery directly to your customer under your company name. At the end of the day, you gain the profit from arbitraging between the wholesale price and the retail selling price.

  电子商务是一种互联网业务，涉及商品和服务贸易信息的传递。BigCommerce，Wix，Volusion等着名网站提供网站设计服务。如果企业家没有广泛的编程语言的技能，设计电子商务网站的最佳选择。他们提供的服务和内置应用程序，可定制您的业务需求。选择一个能够轻松满足业务需求的网站设计。然后，您可以专注于网站的营销和销售。亚马逊，阿里巴巴，eBay，Lazada 等在线市场提供了一个庞大用户群的现成平台。仔细选择销售产品类别，以便您的产品很好地服务于特定的市场。这些平台通常收取在线销售的交易费和佣金。如果您希望避免库存工作带来的麻烦，考虑**直运式**。从您收到买方的订单并将其转发给可信任的批发商。批发商将以您的公司名称直接向客户交货。您可以从批发价格和零售价格之间的获得利润。

Sharing Economy 分享经济

The main idea of sharing economic is that the limited resources can be used by different people when the need arises. It helps to prevent asset underutilization. With small one-time payment, people gain access without owning the resources. Sharing economy relies on digital technology to allocate resources efficiently according to the demand. It is the new means of doing business.

分享经济给予人们使用有限的资源。它有助于防止资产利用不足。通过小额一次性付款，人们可以在不拥有资源的情况下获得使用权限。共享经济依赖于**数字技术**，根据需求有效地分配资源。这是开展业务的新方式。

With the advent of mobile, PC applications and Internet network, sharing economy grew significantly. It becomes an integral part of our daily life. Uber, the ride-sharing business utilizing driver personal vehicles to fetch passenger. It helps the driver to earn more money during their spare time. Airbnb provides a platform for cozy homestay as an alternative lodging option to the traveler with a lower budget. At the same time, property owners earn extra income from the rent. Co-working spaces share working office for an entrepreneur with a minimum fee. Providers even offer other infrastructure, secretary service, courier and mailing service, etc. to start up founder. Peer to peer lending and crowdfunding provide alternative funding for individuals and business owners with lower credit requirements to get the necessary funding.

随着移动电话，PC应用和互联网的出现，共享经济显着增长。它成为我们日常生活中不可或缺的一部分。优步，利用私人车辆接载乘客的共享气车业务。这可以帮助司机在业余时间赚更多钱。Airbnb为旅客提供了舒适的寄宿家庭住宿平台，作为预算较低的旅客的另类选择。与此同时，业主从租金中获得额外收入。共同工作空间以最低费用为企业家共享办公室。供应商甚至提供其他基础设施，秘书服务，快递和邮寄服务等为创始人带来便利。同行借贷和众筹为具有较低信贷要求的个人和企业提供替代资金，让他们获得必要的资金。

Co-creation is a unique form of sharing economy. It involves the participation of end users and relevant stakeholders, in the development process of the final output. From the identification of the problem to implementation of the solution, end-users play the main role create output according to their context. The co-creation process generally takes two important steps. Firstly, users submit their contribution to the company. Secondly, the company selects the most appealing ideas as their final output. At the end of the process, the company developed a more customer-centric output to the market. On the other hand, the end users gained either a one-time prize or even co-ownership rights of the final output. Thus, it is a win-win strategy for both parties in the long run.

共同创造是一种独特的共享经济形式。它是最终用户和企业共同研发产品的模式。从问题的识别到解决方案的实施，最终用户扮演着主要角色。共同创建过程通常需要两个重要步骤。首先,用户向公司提交他们的提案。公司选择最具潜力的提案研发新产品。在过程结束时,企业开发了一种更以客户为中心的产品。另一方面,最终用户获得了一次性奖励甚至产品的共同所有权。因此,从长远来看,这对双方来说都是双赢的策略。

Increasing competition from sharing economy firms has forced many incumbents to revamp current business models and finding innovative ways to bring value to their customers. The value proposition can be delivered via the sharing economy benefiting the owner of the resource, platform provider and its consumer.

共享经济公司的竞争迫使许多老牌企业改变现有的商业模式,并寻找创新方法为客户创造价值。价值主张可以通过共享经济来实现，这样有利于资源所有者，平台提供商及其消费者。

Experience Economy 体验经济

　　Experiences often come with services, but experiences are a distinct form of economic offering, as services are mostly related to the offering of goods together with it. An experience happens when a company utilizes the service as the platform, and goods as tools, to engage consumers in a pleasant and unforgettable event. Experiences are unique. Consumers gain different experiences as the results of the interaction between their inner-mind and the event. The value propositions are delivered in a unique way to the consumers. Consumption of music industry evolves rapidly from the album records to digital format.

　　　　经验通常伴随着服务，是一种独特的经济形式。当企业利用服务作为平台，商品作为工具，让消费者参与愉快和难忘的活动时，就会出现一种体验。这种经验是独一无二的。消费者获得不同的体验，因为他们的内心和活动的相互作用的结果。价值主张需以独特的方式传递给消费者。音乐产业的消费从专辑销售迅速发展到数字格式。

  As the singer gains popularity, the concert can be held as staging experience to audiences. Nowadays, most lucrative incomes for most famous singers are revenues from the mega concert. Tickets charge at premium price generated more revenues than conventional record sales. Experience economy selling a service more than its basic form. Consumers perceive the unique experiences as an offer more than its monetary worth. Most singers staging their talent as a variety show more than just singing in a concert. So, the consumers often willing to pay more to engage in real-life experience more than any virtual world interaction.

　　当歌手越来越受欢迎，音乐会可以作为观众的舞台体验。如今，大多数着名歌手的最赚钱收入来自大型音乐会。以昂贵价格收取门票产生的收入超过传统唱片销售。体验经济销售远远超过其基本形式的服务。消费者将独特的体验视为一种超出其价值的享受。大多数歌手音乐会上演唱和秀出个人才艺。因此，比起任何虚拟世界的消费，歌迷往往愿意支付更多费用参与现实体验的演唱会。

Freemium Economy 免费增值经济

　　Freemium business model is common in-service industry where free users enjoy the basic features of the offering. Only the premium users pay the nominal fee to enjoy the additional features of the service. For instance, Linkedin is a free professional social service platform, the company targeting different category of consumers such as job applicants, employers, advertisers, and headhunters to entice them to pay for the service.

免费增值业务模式是常见的在线行业，免费用户可以享受该产品的基本功能。只有高级用户支付费用才能享受服务的附加功能。例如，Linkedin是一个免费的专业社交服务平台，该公司针对不同类别的消费者，如求职者，雇主，广告商和猎头公司，以吸引他们支付服务费用。

Another form of the freemium company doesn't really charge the users; they charge the advertisers in the business model. Ordinary Facebook users enjoy the social media platform for free, while the businesses pay the advertisement fee to Facebook. Google is another good example of a freemium company. Users search online content with no cost, but the businesses pay the advertisement fee to appear on the top search list.

另一种形式的免费增值公司并没有真正向用户收费。他们向商业模式中的广告商收取费用。普通 Facebook 用户免费享受社交媒体平台，而商家则向 Facebook 支付广告费。谷歌是免费增值公司的一个很好的例子。用户可以免费搜索在线内容，但是企业支付广告费以显示在热门搜索列表中。

Freemium company generally requires a large base of consumers to promote their offering. For the survival of the company, they must maintain a certain level of conversion rate to cover the marginal cost per user. Thus, entrepreneurs need to create the value proposition optimizing the features for free and paid user according to their budget.

免费增值公司通常需要大量消费者来推广他们的产品。为了公司的生存，他们必须保持一定的转换率以涵盖每个用户的边际成本。因此，创业者创造必须根据自己的预算优化免费和付费用户的功能。

Influencer Economy 影响者经济

Influencer economy is a form of marketing using the credibility of influential people to attract consumers. They can reach many consumers via direct or indirect interaction on online or offline media as their "idol." As these people have influence over potential customers' opinion and their purchase decision based on trust.

影响者经济是一种营销形式，利用有影响力的人的信誉来吸引消费者。他们可以通过在线或离线媒体上的直接或间接与"偶像"互动来为商家提高销售。影响者对潜在客户的意见和购买决策有一定的影响力。

Influencer economy depends on how many followers whom an influencer connects with. The impact on purchase decision is stronger when the influencer making more frequent contact with their follower. The credibility and expertise are higher when the influencer is the subject matter expert, which in turn translated into sales. The persuasiveness of the influencer also plays a big role in consumer buying intention.

影响者经济取决于影响者的追随者数量。当影响者与其追随者进行更频繁的接触时，对购买决策的影响更大。当影响者是领域专家时，可信度和专业知识更高，可转化为更高的销售。影响者的说服力也在消费者购买意愿中起着重要作用。

Branding using Corporate Social Responsibility (CSR) 企业社会责任

CSR initiatives build customer loyalty based on high moral and ethical values. Some companies use CSR as a strategic tool to gain customer support for their presence in global markets, helping them achieve the competitive advantage by using social contributions as a form of publicity.

企业社会责任倡议建立在高道德和道德价值观基础上建立客户的忠诚度。一些公司将企业社会责任作为一种战略工具，为其在全球市场中的存在获得客户支持，将社会贡献作为一种宣传形式帮助他们获得竞争优势。

CSR activities can be implemented via charities' activity like sponsoring causes and disadvantaged groups such as disabled people; women; children; refugees; minorities; indigenous peoples; migrant workers; elderly groups, etc. CSR initiatives can also practice via an environmentally friendly approach. It helps to reduce waste and pollution of our planet. "Green" manufacturing emphasizes utilizing renewable energy to reduce the carbon footprint; reusing and recycling to reduce waste, minimizing natural resource and pollution to the environment.

企业社会责任活动可以通过慈善活动来实施，如赞助弱势群体，残疾人市，女性，儿童，难民，少数民族，原住民，农民工。企业社会责任倡议也可以通过环保方法实践。它有助于减少我们地球的浪费和污染。"绿色"制造业利用再生能源来减少碳足迹，循环，重复使用。以减少浪费自然资源和对环境的污染。

Instead of prioritizing profit, CSR initiatives emphasize people, planet, and profit. It is a comprehensive approach to achieve competitiveness and sustainable growth at the same time. The company emphasizes on CSR initiatives create unique value propositions that enticing conscious consumers in modern society.

企业社会责任倡议不是优先考虑利润，而是强调人，地球和利润。这是实现竞争力和可持续增长的综合方法。强调企业社会责任倡议可创造独特的价值主张，吸引现代社会中有良好意识的消费者。

Scarcity 稀缺感

People value a resource as precious when they find it difficult to get access to it. The law of supply and demand explains the interaction between the supply and the demand for a resource. Generally, low supply and high demand raise the price. On the contrary, ample supply and poor demand cause the price to fall. For instance, airfare during peak season is more expensive than off peak-season. We may focus on how to create this phenomenon changing the customer's perception of value.

当人们发现很难获得资源时，他们会认为这些资源是相对宝贵的。供求定律解释了供给与资源需求之间的相互作用。通常，低供应和高需求会提高价格。相反，供应充足和需求不足导致价格下跌。例如，旺季期间的机票价格比淡季期间的机票贵。我们必须关注如何创造这种现象，从而改变客户对价值的看法。

For products, entrepreneurs may sell the products far away from the source of its origin. A higher price can be charged at the inland city-center seafood restaurant than a coastal restaurant. The retailer charges a premium price on imported products or sells to overseas market.

企业家可出售远离其来源的产品。内陆市中心海鲜餐厅的价格高于沿海餐厅。零售商对进口产品和海外市场销售收取溢价。

Limited time offer creates a sense of scarcity. It creates a sense of urgency of the customer to purchase within the promotion period. Limited resources also trigger the purchase intention. Low quantity indicates the item is fast moving. People will be tempted to do the purchase before the item sold out. The pre-release marketing campaign is another way to create a sense of scarcity. Smartphone manufacturer such as Apple using the pre-order sales to generate hype before the actual release of the products. This strategy also enables the producer to estimate the demand for the new phone.

限时优惠会产生稀缺感。它在促销期内创造了顾客购买的紧迫感。有限的资源也会触发购买意向。数量少表示物品畅销。在物品售罄之前，人们很想购买。预发布营销活动是另一种营造稀缺感的方式。Apple 等智能手机制造商使用预购销售在产品实际发布之前炒作。此策略让生产者能够估计新手机的需求。

Mass customization of products/services based on customer preference also another form of scarcity marketing. When the outputs are exclusive to the customer, it creates what the customer really wants. Customers often willing to pay more since it changes the perception of value on their mind with the exclusive product. It might have great influence on emotional attachment, which in turn affected loyalty on the products/services.

基于客户偏好的产品大规模定制也是另一种形式的稀缺营销。当产品专属于客户时，它会创建客户真正想要的东西。客户通常愿意支付更多费用，因为它会通过独家产品改变他们对价值的看法。顾客可能会对独特商品感产生心里上的依恋，从而影响对产品/品牌的忠诚度。

Cultural elements 文化元素

Language can be either spoken or written. One of the most crucial developments in the civilized society was the creation of written language. If you wish to introduce the product to a foreign country, you may need to find a translator to do the translation for the marketing materials. It is important that the value proposition can be delivered as intended in the context of the foreign language.

语言可以是口语或书面语。书面语言是文明社会最重要的创造之一。如果您希望将产品介绍到国外，您可能需要找一名翻译来进行营销翻译。价值主张可以在外语的背景下按传递原文的意向。

Cultural norms are the standards and expectations for behaving in society. Formal norms are the most important standard of behavior in any society as governed by the rule of law. In most countries, it includes criminal law, civil law, traffic laws. Informal norms refer as standards of behavior that are less important such as the folkway and custom. Mannerisms are everyday behaviors as how we interact with people. It is one example of informal norms. A good business value proposition must not go against any social norms of society.

文化规范是社会行为的标准。正式规范是任何社会中最重要的行为标准并受法治支配。在大多数国家，它包括刑法，民法，交通法。非正式规范指的是次要的行为标准，如民俗和习俗。习俗是人与人们互动的日常行为。这是非正式规范的一个例子。一个好的商业价值主张绝不能违背任何社会规范。

Different cultures have rituals, or established procedures, ceremonies and festive seasons according to their own calendar. Value propositions deliver via cultural elements create more business opportunities in the diverse ethnic group in the market.

不同的文化有不同的仪式，节日和庆典。通过这些文化元素可以在市场中的不同种族群中创造更多商机。

The framework of Value Proposition 价值主张的框架

The framework of the value proposition is summarized in a concise table, using the consumer's buying experience (i.e. from purchase until disposal), and modern elements value proposition that we discussed before. It helps entrepreneurs identify important elements to create a compelling value proposition. This framework also creates a unique selling proposition to consumers.

Value Propposition Design Products/Services	Utility	New Economy Model	Cultural Elements	CSR initiatives	Scarcity
Purchase	Price: High/Medium/Low	E-commerce- online store Sharing Economy- using online apps to allocate resources	Different language marketing material Festive offer	Contribution to charity and vulnerable group	Pre order- create sense of anticipation Limited offer- create the sense of urgency to buy
Using the product/service	Productivity- Increase the productive effort and performance Prestige- Pride to user Durability-Withstand pressure, damage,wear and tear Design- Savvy and elegant Convenience- easy to use, hassle free Low risk- harmless to user	Sharing Economy- prevent underutilization of resources Influencer economy- entice user using influential people Experience economy- create unique user experience Freemium model- free basic features for most user Co-Creation model- create new product/ service from user's idea	Different language product/service Not against any law & social norm	Envrionmental friendly Low carbon Foot print, zero emission No harm to user physically or mentally	Mass Customization- create unique product/service for customer
After sales service	Exchange and refund policy Warranty(on site/ off site) Complaint and feedback	Co-Creation model- improve product from customer feedback	Different language support	Reliability and quality of product and service	Individual solution for customer
Disposal	Easy to dispose No Extra Cost	Sharing economy- sharing the unwanted items for recycling, or others in need	Cultural access and attitude toward recyling and waste management	Recylable & Reusable material	Special disposal service for customer

价值主张的框架总结在一个简明的表格中，使用消费者的购买经验（即从购买到**弃置**），以及我们之前讨论过的现代元素价值主张。它帮助企业家识别重要元素，以创造引人注目的价值主张。该框架也为消费者创造了独特的价值。

价值主张设计产品与服务	效用	新经济模式	文化元素	企业社会责任	稀缺性
采购	价格：高/中/低	电子商务 - 在线商店 共享经济 - 使用在线应用程序分配费费	不同的语言和材料 节日优惠	对慈善机构和弱势群体的贡献	预订 - 创造期待感 有限的报价 - 创造购买的紧迫感
使用产品/服务	生产力 - 增加主生产力和绩效 耐久性 - 承受压力，损坏、磨损 设计 - 精致优雅 方便 - 易于使用，无忧无虑 低风险 - 对用户无害	共享经济 - 防止资源利用不足 影响经济的用户使用有影响力的人 体验经济 - 创造独特的用户体验 免费增值模型 - 大多数用户可以使用的基本功能 共创模型 - 根据用户的想法去创造新产品服务	不同的语言产品/服务 不是反任何法律和社会规范	环境友好 低碳足迹 - 零排放 对身体或精神上的用户无害	大规模定制 - 为客户创造独特的购买的服务
售后服务	交换和退款 保修（现场/非现场） 投诉和反馈	共同创建模型 - 从客户反馈中改进产	不同的语言支持	产品和服务的可靠性和质量	为客户提供个性化服务
处置	易于处理 没有额外费用	共享经济 - 分享不需要的物品以及其他需要的人 供回收，喊其他有需要的人	文化对废物处理的态度	可循环和可重复使用的材料	为客户提供然处置服务

Chapter 4 -Customer 第四章 - 客户

Customer Segmentation 客户细分

Generally, there are two approaches to marketing. In the undifferentiated strategy, all customers are targeted using one marketing strategy, without any specific efforts to serve any groups. A single marketing mix is implemented using the same price, product, placement, and similar promotional effort - to gain most of the consumers in the mass market. This may work only when the product/service is universal with the standard feature.

有两种营销方法。在无差别的策略中，所有客户都使用一种营销策略。使用相同的价格，产品，布局和类似的促销努力实现单一营销组合，以获得大众市场中的大多数消费者。这可能仅在大众产品/服务的时才有效。

In today's competitive market, entrepreneurs often need to focus on several customer segments with differentiated strategy. From the segmentation, entrepreneurs can determine the profit of each section of customer by analyzing its revenues and costs. With the information, the necessary resources can be allocated to marketing activity, to match the needs of different customer segments. The segment performances must be evaluated so that the new plan can be made according to the market conditions over time. The appropriate customer segmentations allow the entrepreneurs to understand on how to satisfy the needs of customers, predict their future purchase decision, allocate the required resources, identify opportunities to optimize the marketing campaign, monitor growth patterns of important customers and track sales performance over time.

在当今竞争激烈的市场中，企业家需要差异化的营销策列服务多个客户群。通过细分，企业家可以通过分析收入和成本来确定每个客户的利润。利用这些信息，可以将必要的资源分配给营销活动，以满足不同客户群的需求。必须评估表现，以便可以根据市场状况随时推出销售计划。适当的客户细分使企业家能够了解如何满足不同客户群的需求，预测他们未来的购买趋势，分配所需的资源，配合营销活动，掌握重要客户的增长率以及销售业绩。

Proper customer segmentation helps entrepreneurs to build distribution channels, design products or services features, determine pricing strategy to suit the needs of a different segment of consumers. Thus, customer segmentation is important to subdivide the market into meaningful segments, according to their geographic, demographic, psychographic and behavioral profiles.

　　适当的客户细分有助于企业家建立分销渠道，设计产品或服务功能，确定定价策略以满足不同消费群体的需求。因此，根据客户的地理，人口统计，心理和行为概况，客户细分对于将市场细分是非常重要的。

Geographic segmentation 地里分化

　　Geographic segmentation segregates markets according to geographical features. segmentation subdivided to state Entrepreneurs can divide markets from as vast as continents to be as small as postcode or even street address. Geographic segmentation is common in international marketing where marketers decide their offering according to countries. Geographical, city, town, population density, and climatic zone are also example of geographical segmentation. By combining demographic and geographic segmentation, geo-demographic segregation may derive more insights from a different group of consumers.

地理分割根据地理特征细分市场。细分可以将市场从大陆划分为至邮政编码甚至街道地址一样小的市场。地理分割在国际营销中很常见，营销人员根据国家/地区决定其产品。地理，城市，城镇，人口密度和气候带也是地理分割的例子。通过结合人口统计和地理分割，地理人口统计学的细分可以从不同的消费者群体中获得更多的见解。

Demographic segmentation 人口统计细分

Demographic segregation divides consumers according to the structure of the population. The demographic profiles such as age, gender, income, occupation, race, marital status, family size, etc. are among the common structure of a population. Consumers with the same profile often exhibit similar purchasing habit that translating into preferences on products or services. Practically, demographic segmentation can be done using those variables available on the national census study.

人口统计学细分根据人口结构划分消费者。年龄，性别，收入，职业，种族，婚姻状况，家庭规模等人口统计资料属于人口统计的项目。具有相同概况的消费者通常表现出类似的购买习惯，转化为对产品或服务的偏好。一般上，可以使用国家人口普查研究中的变量进行人口统计的细分。

Psychographic segmentation 心理细分

Psychographics is a combination of psychology and demographics of consumers. Psychographic information is the psychology of consumers who derive from the structure of the population. Demographics explain the dry facts from the structure of the population, while psychographics describes the purchase behavior that derives from the demographics of consumers. Entrepreneurs can only reach the target consumers when they understand both demographics and psychology of the consumers. It is necessary applying the rule of association to link both types of data.

心理细分心理学和消费者人口统计学的结合。心理信息是源于人口结构和消费者的心理信息。人口统计学从人口结构中解读，而消费者心理数据则描述了源自消费者人口统计的购买行为。企业家只有了解消费者的人口统计和心理，才能接触到目标消费者。有必要应用关联规则来链接两种类型的数据。

Lifestyle elements like activities, interests, and opinions also affect consumers purchase decision. Different consumers might have distinct preferences on **activities and interests** based on their education level. If the more educated consumers like reading, they might choose diverse genres based on their own interest and professional background. Thus, activities, interests, and opinions inform us a lot about a consumer's purchase decision.

活动，兴趣和意见等生活方式元素也会影响消费者的购买决策。不同的消费者可能根据他们的教育水平对不同的活动和兴趣有偏好。受过更多教育的消费者喜欢阅读，他们可能会根据自己的兴趣和专业背景选择不同的类型的刊物。因此，活动，兴趣和意见告诉我们很多影响消费者的购买决策的因素。

Consumers can be categorized into different social classes. This depends mainly on their purchasing power. It is also affected by the occupation, income as well as their spending habits. Consumers always buy what they can afford to maintain their social class. Therefore, premium brands target wealthy consumers because only these people would be the classes capable of buying their products. It often needs to emphasize lifestyle, social class, and branding.

消费者可以来至不同的社会阶层。这主要取决于他们的购买能力。消费能力也受到职业，收入和消费习惯的影响。消费者总是购买维持个人社会阶层象征的产品。因此，优质品牌瞄准富裕消费者，因为只有这些人才能够购买他们的产品。高端品牌往往需要强调生活方式，社会阶层和品牌。

Behavioral Segmentation 行为细分

Behavioral segmentation segregates the consumers based on patterns of behavior displayed from the purchase record. It allows businesses to divide consumers into the categories according to the attitude, response when consuming a product or service. Common behavioral variables include purchase history such as purchase frequency based on the number of purchases in a certain period.

行为细分根据消费者从公司购买记录显示的行为来细分消费者。企业根据态度，消费产品或服务时的回馈将消费者划分为类别。常见的行为变量包括购买历史，例如特定时期内的购买数量的购买频率。

User status is another option to classify customers by their relationship with the business. It can be subdivided into festive consumers, non-festive consumers based on purchase records. The behavior classification on users' status can also be members, non-members, one-time users, regular users depend on their interaction with the business.

用户状态是根据客户与业务关系对客户进行分类的另一种选择。它可以根据购买记录细分为季节性消费者，非季节性节日消费者。用户状态的行为分类也可以是成员，非成员，一次性用户，常期用户。这取决于他们与生意上的往来关系。

Through behavioral data, customers can be subdivided by loyalty based on purchase history. Loyal customers are the biggest sales contributors & brand advocates. They are the perfect target group for loyalty programs that offer special privileges, rewards, and discount, to strengthen the customer relationship and incentivize continued future business. Thus, from an economic point of view, it is relatively cheaper to retain them than acquire a new customer.

通过行为数据，可以根据客户的购买历史进行细分。忠诚的客户群是最大的销售贡献者和品牌拥护者。他们是会员计划的完美目标群体，提供特殊优惠，奖励和折扣，以加强忠诚客户关系并创造未来商机。因此，从经济角度来看，保留忠诚客户比获得新客户更有商业价值。

Interest-based behavioral segmentation is important to deliver personalized experiences that keep customers coming back for more purchases. It is applicable whether your aim is to increase product consumption, cross-sell or up-sell to your consumers, or deliver the marketing content and facilitate them to purchase more. One of the greatest advantages of interest behavior is the ability to connect specific interests with the intent of purchase.

兴趣的行为细分对于提供个性化体验非常重要，这些体验可以让客户回来购买更多产品。无论您的目标是增加产品消费，交叉销售，还是提供营销内容并促进他们购买欲，兴趣细分最大优势之一是能够将个人喜好与购买意图联系起来。

Machine learning can help to scale the process. As an increasing number of consumers engage and interact, there will be more interest-based data capture and learn over time to produce more accurate suggestion in the recommender system. Netflix, Amazon, and Google use recommendation system for suggesting content and products based on customers' interests. Each time you collect customers' data, you may associate with the number of additional potential interests, that might be effective for engaging customer with related products using the collaborative filtering approach. Using the behavioral segmentation methods described above, you can make marketing campaigns more efficient, maximize ROI, increase customer lifetime value and build a deeper knowledge to retain your customer.

机器学习可以帮助简化细分过程。随着越来越多的消费者的数据累计和分析，机器学习的推荐系统中可提供更准确的建议。Netflix，亚马逊和 Google 根据客户的兴趣使用推荐系统介绍相关内容和产品。每次收集客户数据时，您都可以使用该客户的兴趣与相关产品的关联以销售产品。使用上述行为细分方法，您可以提高营销活动的效率，最大化投资回报率，提高客户的生命周期价值，并建立更深入的知识来留住您的客户。

Customer Relationship 客户关系

Customer relationship management (CRM) is an approach to manage the entire customer relationship, including the purchase process, post-sales service, feedback and recommendations to all customers. It aims to improve business relationships with customers, particularly focusing on **customer retention** and ultimately driving sales growth. CRM must be pragmatic in terms of scale and budget. Launching highly focused projects with narrow scopes and modest goals is a more practical approach. Entrepreneurs must be investing heavily in solving clearly defined problems within the customer relationship cycle—the activities that run from the segmenting and targeting of customers all the way through to retain them.

客户关系管理（CRM）是一种管理整个客户关系的方法，包括购买流程，售后服务，反馈和对所有客户的建议。它旨在改善与客户的关系，并关注客户保留与推动销售增长。 CRM 在规模和预算方面必须务实。启动有目标的客户群和高度集中的 CRM 项目是一种更实用的方法。企业家必须投资在 CRM 项目以实现客户的细分和定位到保留原有客户的活动。以解决客户关系周期中明确的问题。

In a larger firm, customer relationships are handled by the customer service department in the form of employee-customer interaction. Personal assistance is assigned during sales and/or after sales for a company with bigger budget to foster a better relationship with the customer. For a start-up, an entrepreneur can offer dedicated private assistance to the customer. It is the most intimate and hands-on personal assistance in which the entrepreneur or sales personnel is assigned to handle all the inquiries and needs of clients. It requires more effort and time, but it helps to nurture the relationship with customers and retain them over time.

在较大的公司中，客户关系由客户服务部门以员工－客户互动的形式处理。在销售和/或售后期间为预算较大的公司分配个人协助，以促进与客户的更好关系。对于初创企业，企业家可以为客户提供专门的客服和售后服务。这是最直接和有效的方法，企业家或销售人员直接处理客户的所有询问和售后服务。它需要更多的努的力和时间，但它有助于培养与建立客户的关系并有效地保留原有的客户。

Create a community facilitating the interactions among the customers and company. The community platform sharing knowledge and solving problems between customers via **social listening**. It requires regular and consistent efforts such as monitoring conversations, analyzing feedbacks, answering questions and solving issues. Co-creation is viable in an active community where the member input is incorporated into the final output of the company. The community members can research the products/services, engage with others to solve issues and post comments on the output. These communities are the best way to create customer-centric output. It is also a method to empower the customers to serve themselves and make them feel connected with the communities and loyal to your brand.

创建一个促进客户和公司之间互动的社区。社区平台通过社交倾听，分享知识并解决客户的问题。它需要定期和一致的努力，如观察对话，分析反馈，回答问题和解决问题。共同创造在活跃的社区中是可行的，其中成员设计或想法被纳入公司生产商品的考量。社区成员可以研究产品/服务，与他人互动以解决问题并在平台上发表评论。这些社区是创建以客户为中心的产品的最佳方式。它也是一种让客户能够为公司服务并让他们与社区保持联系并忠诚于您的品牌的方法。

Chapter 5 Channels 渠道

A company can deliver its value proposition to different segments of customers via its own or partner channel. Productive channels will generate a company's sales in ways that are quick, inexpensive and efficient. Channel management is a method of trading, delivering your products using various marketing and sales technique to reach possible customers. A business must determine the goal of each channel and define the specific framework for each of the channels to produce the desired results. Identifying the customer segment linked to each channel also helps to determine the best products/ services to pitch to those channels.

公司可以通过自己或合作伙伴渠道向

不同的客户群提供价产品或服务。有效的渠道将以快速，廉价和高效的方式产生公司的销售。渠道管理是一各种营销和销售产品的管道，以吸引客户和创造销售。企业必须确定每个渠道的目标，并为每个渠道定义特定的框架，以产生预期的结果。识别每个渠道的客户群也有助于确定向这些渠道推销的最佳产品/服务给不同的客户群。

Channel Strategy 渠道策略

A channel strategy is the action plan for reaching customers with products and services. The design of the channel plan must consider factors such as customer preference; competitor in the market; constraints such as costs, resources, and capabilities. Proper channel strategy aims to develop a relationship with customers to gain repeat sales and increases the profitability of an existing customer. The successful channel strategy often streamlines communication between the business and customer. To achieve this, the segmentation is important for selection of the target group. After the selection, the right marketing mix with the customized channel can be delivered to serve the customer better. The objective of channel management is to establish direct communication with customers in each channel. If the company achieves this goal, it creates the best marketing channels that suit with diverse customer segment. The techniques utilized in every channel could be different, but the overall strategy must deliver the value proposition of business consistently.

渠道策略是通过产品和服务吸引客户的行动计划。渠道计划的设计必须考虑的因素如：市场竞争者，成本，资源和企业的能力。适当的渠道策略旨在与客户建立关系，以获得重复销售并从现有客户中提升盈利。成功的渠道策略通常简化了企业与客户之间的沟通。为实现此目的，选择目标客户群很重要。选择之后，可以提供与定制渠道的正确营销组合，以更好地为客户服务。渠道管理的目标是让每个渠道的客户建立直接沟通。如果公司实现这一目标，它将创建适合不同客户群的最佳营销渠道。每个渠道执行的方法可能不同，但总体战略必须一致地实现企业的价值主张。

Direct Channel 直接渠道

Brick and click model 上下线模式

  Entrepreneurs who are product manufacturers or service providers have a few channel options. The easiest way is the direct channel in which they sell to the customer without any intermediary channels. Opening physical store by locating near customers is one of the choices. For example, a pharmaceutical company that sells medicinal products can locate sales offices near major hospitals and clinics. The suppliers may also employ a sales force to close deals with customers or sell its products or services through e-commerce websites, mobile applications. Direct selling via door to door represents another option, although this business model has been replaced by e-commerce. Combining your online and offline business such that they complement with each other as bricks and clicks model. For instance, physical stores may be used for delivery and after-sales service for web orders. On the other hands, the e-commerce store can be used by the retail store to extend inventory, product range and expand customer base beyond the geographical reach.

产品制造商或服务业有一些特定的渠道选择。最简单的方法是在没有任何中间渠道的情况下向客户销售的直接渠道。直接在定位客户群附近开设实体店是其中一个选择。例如，销售医药产品的制药公司可以在主要医院和诊所附近设立销售办事处。供应商还可以聘请销售人员与客户达成交易，或通过电子商务网站，移动应用程序销售其产品或服务。通过门到门的直接销售代表了另一种选择，尽管这种商业模式渐渐地被电子商务所取代。结合您的在线和离线业务，使他们互补成为网路和实体店结合的模式。例如，实体店可用于网络订单的交付和售后服务。另一方面，零售商店可以使用电子商务商店来扩展库存，产品范围并服务超出地理范围限制的客户群体。

Dropship model 直运模式

  Recently, a new type of online retailer known as "drop shipper" has become very popular, especially to the individual seller. Drop shipper is a retailer who doesn't keep any stock but generates online sales and earns commission from the wholesale supplier. The biggest advantage of this retail fulfillment method is that the entrepreneur doesn't have to bear the expenses on inventory and other related overhead costs of a traditional retailer. Drop shipper simply passes the order to the wholesale partner who handles the product delivery and takes a commission from the sales. eCommerce business that runs on a drop shipping model is largely dependent on wholesale suppliers and needs to be careful about sourcing the credible partner.

最近，一种被称为"直运模式"的新型在线零售商变得非常受欢迎，特别是对个人卖家而言。 Drop shipper 是零售商，但不会有任何库存，并能在线销售并从批发供应商处获得佣金。这种零售方法的最大优点是企业家不必承担传统零售商的库存和其他相关间接成本的费用。卖家只需将订单传递给处理产品交付的批发合作伙伴，并从销售中获得佣金。以直接运输模式运行的电子商务业务在很大程度上依赖于批发供应商，因此需要谨慎采购和选择可靠的合作伙伴。

Omnichannel 全方位渠道

Omnichannel is a cross-channel integration business model that companies deploy to improve the overall customer experience. Rather than working in isolation, all channels and the supporting units are designed to cooperate with each other. To deploy omnichannel, the action plan does not need to incorporate all available channels, which is impractical. Instead, it involves the integration of all channels using available resources and capabilities such that the customer experience across multiple channels is pleasant and efficient than using single channel independently.

Omnichannel 是一种跨渠道集成业务模式，公司可以部署这种模式以改善整体客户体验。所有渠道和支撑单位都相互配合，而不是孤立地工作。要部署全渠道，行动计划不需要包含所有市场上的可用渠道，这是不切实际的。相反，它涉及企业可用资源集成所有渠道，使跨渠道的客户体验比独立使用单个渠道更愉快和有效。

  It is important to incorporate the multiple channels as one cohesive strategy that creates the integrated customer experience. For instance, the customer can be shopping in a physical store, the online store from a desktop or mobile device, or by social media, or by telephone, and the experience would be seamless from any channels.

  多个渠道合并为一个有凝聚力的平台，并创造整合的客户体验是至关重要的商业战略。例如，顾客可以在实体店，在线商店从桌面，移动设备，社交媒体，电话购物，可以从任何渠道享受同样的体验。

Omnichannel has wide applications across various industries such as healthcare, financial services, government agency, telecom, and retail industries. Companies that utilize omnichannel often need to create a unique selling proposition that engages with customers via multiple avenues simultaneously.

Omnichannel 广泛应用于医疗保健，金融服务，政府机构，电信和零售行业等各个行业。利用全渠道的公司通常需要创建一个独特的销售主张，通过多个途径同时与客户互动。

Indirect channels-Distribution Partners 间接渠道 - 分销合作伙伴

Value-added sellers 增值卖家

Entrepreneurs can also generate sales via indirect channels involving one or more intermediaries. They can sell via value-added seller (VARs). VARs are companies that bundle different products and services and resale them as a turn-key solution to end users. It is referred to as one tier distribution system since it involves only one level of the middleman. In the two-tier distribution system, the entrepreneur sells to wholesaler/distributor, which, in turn sells to VARs and finally to the end user.

企业家还可以通过涉及一个或多个中介的间接渠道创造销售。他们可以通过增值卖家（VAR）进行销售。 VAR是捆绑不同产品和服务的公司，并将其作为最终用户提供解决方案进行转售。在一层分配系统，它只涉及VAR作为中间人。在双层分销系统中，企业家向批发商销售，批发商再销售给VAR，最后才售卖给最终用户。

The value can be created by customizing, integrating, consulting, training and implementation of professional services. The value can also be added by customizing the application for the product designed for the customer's preference which is then resold as a new package. For instance, VARs develop platform software to incorporate other vendors' software packages.

　　VAR 可以通过定制，集成，咨询，培训和实施专业服务来创造附加价值。还可以通过自客户定义的的产品或应用程序来提升价值，然后将其转售为新的产品。例如，VAR 开发不同平台的软件以让其他供应商的软件包使用。

　　The term turnkey is often used in the IT industry, where a company purchases all the necessary components and builds a fully operational system for end users. By doing this, the company has added value above the cost of the individual components and sells it at the premium price to end users.

Customers would purchase the system from the reseller if they don't have time and skill to assemble the entire system themselves.

术语 Turnkey 通常用于 IT 行业，VAR 公司购买所有必要的组件并为最终用户构建完全可操作的系统。通过这样，公司增加了超过单个组件成本的价值，并以更高的价格向最终用户出售。如果客户没有时间和技能自己组装整个系统，客户将从 VAR 购买系统。

Wholesaler 批发商

The wholesaler is a middleman that buys in large quantities from a supplier or producer and resells at a wholesale price to a retailer. An entrepreneur with excess production capacity may choose to sell in bulk quantity to the wholesaler. Wholesalers normally specialize in a certain type of product or sell a broad range of stocks to retailers in different industries. A wholesaler that only stock non-competing products for a brand are known as sole distributors. Besides breaking bulk quantities orders into a smaller package, wholesalers can also assemble or package goods as part of the value-added process to the retailer. Wholesalers typically store products in a warehouse for shorter periods of time compared to distributors.

  批发商从供应商或生产商那里大量购买，并以批发价格转售给零售商。生产能力过剩的企业家可以选择批量销售给批发商。批发商通常专注于某种类型的产品，或向不同行业的零售商销售各种各样的产品。仅为莫种品牌销售的批发商被称为独家代理授权商。除了将批量分成较小的包装外，批发商还可以将货物作为增值流程的一部分组装或包装给零售商。与零售商相比，批发商通常将产品存放在仓库中的时间较短。

Licensing 许可证贸易

Licensing enables an entrepreneur to access the broader customer base instantly by leveraging existing production, distribution, and marketing systems that other companies build over time. Licensing fees typically amount to only a small percentage of royalty, but it can add up substantially when the volume of sales is large. The intellectual property owner (licensor) must ensure that the partner (licensee) has the resources, capabilities, and commitment to deliver the product or service with the same capacity as the owner. Intellectual property licensing is common in the industry such as broadcasting, publication, software, academia and high-tech industry involving technology transfer.

许可证贸易使企业家能够利用其他公司的技术随时提升的现有生产，分销和营销系统，立即销售给更广泛的客户群。许可费通常只占特许权使用费的一小部分，但是当销售量很大时，它可能会大幅增加。知识产权所有者（许可方）必须确保合作伙伴（被许可方）拥有能力提供相符的素质的产品，以维护许可方的商誉。知识产权许可在一些行业中很常见，如广播，出版，软件，学术和涉及技术转让的高科技产业。

  A licensor also may grant permission to a licensee to use the trademark or brand without the fear of infringement claim from the licensor. With the license, the licensee can use the trademark to gain the established market share. The license often depends on specific contractual terms such as a geographic region, a period of time or certain scope of business.

  许可人也可以允许被许可人使用商标或品牌，而不必担心许可人的侵权索赔。通过许可证贸易，被许可人可以使用该商标获得既定的市场份额。许可证通常取决于特定的合同条款，例如地理区域，时间或某些业务范围。

Franchising 特许经营

  Franchising is a special form of licensing, which can be divided into two main categories. In a product distribution model, the franchisor sells finished products to the franchisee and permits them to use their brand and trademark. In return, the franchisees buy a minimum order of quantity of products or pay fees to the franchisor. Most of the time, the franchisee does not receive the full support to run the business and require developing sales service independently in this model. The product franchise model is quite similar to a supplier-dealer relationship, with a few differences in the relationship. The franchisee may sell products on an exclusive or semi-exclusive basis and receive support from the franchisor. The automobile industry is a typical example of the product distribution franchise.

　　特许经营是一种特殊的经营形式，可分为两大类。在产品分销模式中，特许人将成品销售给特许经营商，并允许他们使用其品牌和商标。作为回报，特许经营商向特许人购买产品或支付费用。大多数情况下，特许经营商并未获得运营业务的全部支持，并且需要在此模式中独立开发销售服务。产品特许经营模式与供应商 - 经销商关系非常相似，但存在一些差异。特许经营商以独家或半独家的方式销售产品，并获得特许人的支持。汽车工业是产品分销特许经营是典型例子。

In business format franchises, the franchisee utilizes franchisor's brand name and trademark. Furthermore, the franchisee gains the complete system of the franchisor including operations, marketing, inventory, support, etc. This model is the more consistent way of achieving sustainable results for the franchisee. The franchisee is often empowered with a detailed plan that entails the entire operation of the franchise. Besides, the franchisee is provided with training and support on advertising, marketing, management of the premises, recruitment, training of staff, and even standard operating procedure of the franchise.

在商业格式特许经营中，特许经营商使用特许人的品牌名称和商标。此外，特许经营商获得了特许经营者的完整系统，包括运营，营销，库存，支持单位等。这种模式是为特许经营者实现可持续结果的更一致的方式。特许经营商经常被赋予详细的计划，该计划涉及特许经营的整个运作。此外，特许经营商在广告，营销，管理，招聘，员工培训，甚至得到特许经营的标准操作的培训和支持。

Original equipment manufacturers (OEMs), managed service providers (MSPs), consultants, systems integrators (SIs), independent software vendor(ISVs) may also serve as indirect channel partners. Entrepreneur pursuing these alternative channels will often need to create a partner program to manage relationships to avoid conflict of interest.

原始设备制造商（OEM），托管服务提供商（MSP），系统集成商（SI），独立软件供应商（ISV）也可以作为间接渠道合作伙伴。使用这些替代渠道的企业家通常需要创建一个合作伙伴计划来管理关系以避免利益冲突。

Original equipment manufacturers (OEM)原始设备制造商

Original Equipment Manufacturer (OEM) is a company that produces parts or equipment that may be sold under another manufacturer brand name. Entrepreneurs with excess manufacturing capacity may choose to be OEM by distributing their products to other companies.

原始设备制造商（OEM）是一家生产其他制造商品牌名称销售零件或设备的公司。制造能力过剩的企业家可以选择当 OEM 将产品分销给其他公司。

OEM is common in software distribution. For example, Microsoft sells the retail version of Windows operating system (OS) to end users via their platform. On the other hand, the OEM version Windows OS often bundled with a personal computer (PC) in the market. Warranty terms might be different for retail and OEM version.

OEM 在软件分发中很常见。例如，Microsoft 通过其平台向最终用户销售零售版 Windows 操作系统（OS）。另一方面，Windows OS 的 OEM 版本通常与个人计算机（PC）一起出售。零售版和 OEM 版的保修条款可能有所不同。

OEM drives down the unit cost of the product by manufacturing bulk quantities to achieve the scale of economies. On the other hand, using OEM products allow the partner company to get the needed products or components without owning and operating a highly complex business activity.

OEM 通过大批量生产来降低产品的单位成本，以实现经济规模。另一方面，使用 OEM 产品允许合作伙伴获得所需的产品或组件，而无需拥有和运营高度复杂的业务活动。

Managed service provider (MSP) 托管服务提供商

A managed service provider (MSP) is a company that manages a client's IT infrastructure or systems, regularly and under a subscription model. MSP often charges for the services under different packages such as per-device, per-user, number of features, projects or all-inclusive pricing. Entrepreneurs may choose to outsource certain business processes that require high cost & expertise to MSP, to expand the existing channel.

　　托管服务提供商（MSP）是一家定期和按订阅模式管理客户的 IT 基础架构或系统公司。MSP 通常会根据不同的模式例如软件包，设备，用户，功能数量，项目或全包价格收取服务费用。企业家可以选择将需要高成本和专业知识的某些业务流程外包给 MSP，以扩展现有渠道。

Systems integrators (SI)系统集成商

　　A system integrator (SI) is a person or company that specializes in integrating components such as hardware, software, networking and so that those subsystems function as an integrated system. Using system integrator, a company can obtain cheaper, pre-configured components and different software as one unified solution to fulfill the business objectives, in contrast to more expensive, customized application that may require unique components or programming skills.

系统集成商（SI）是专门集成诸如硬件，软件，网络之类的组件的人或公司，并且这些子系统用作集成系统。使用系统集成商的产品，公司可以获得更便宜，预配置的组件和不同的软件作为一个统一的解决方案来实现业务目标，而更昂贵的定制应用程序可能需要独特的组件或编程技能。

An integrated solution can also simplify the complex process of sourcing and dealing with multiple vendors. Otherwise, the standalone systems needed to purchase and manage independently. Hence, systems integration reduces the tedious process of both procurement and technical issues. Entrepreneurs may often need SI assistance to do integration across the system of multiple channels.

集成的解决方案还可以简化采购和处理多个供应商的复杂过程。否则，独立系统需要独立购买和管理。因此，系统集成减少了采购和技术问题的繁琐过程。企业家也可能需要 SI 协助来在多个渠道的系统中进行整合。

Independent software vendor (ISV) 独立软件供应商

Generally, the independent software vendors are often the companies that developing software with specialized niche offerings. For Instance, they can focus on making the specific business unit applications (HR, Accounting, IT, Marketing, procurement), or industry software (manufacturer, wholesaler, retailer) software for either goods or service providers. There is also ISV providing a highly customized solution, such as data migration utilities, networking, point of sales system, etc.

  独立软件供应商通常是开发专门产品的软件的公司。他们可以专注于为商品或服务提供特定业务单位应用程序（人力资源，会计，IT，营销，采购）或行业软件（制造商，批发商，零售商）软件。ISV还提供定制的解决方案，例如数据迁移实用程序，网络，销售点系统等。

  An independent software vendor program will generally offer a mix of technical and specialized domain knowledge application for a software platform such as Microsoft, Linux, Google, etc. ISV software may include in areas such as technology training, briefings on product development roadmaps, specific pricing and licensing terms, product discounts and co-marketing initiatives. A platform provider also offers ISV approval seal via software validation programs.

　　独立软件供应商计划通常会为软件平台（如Microsoft，Linux，Google等）提供技术和专业领域知识应用程序。ISV软件可能包括技术培训，产品开发路线图，定价，产品折扣和联合营销计划。平台提供商还通过软件验证程序提供ISV批准印章以鼓励这些软件在平台使用。

Generally, an independent software vendor program operates within a platform of business partner program. Such programs aim to cover a spectrum of partner relationships and interactions to leverage joint strengths, convert them into incremental business opportunities of the platform software. While ISVs customize specialized software that is added to its platform's software, original equipment manufacturers use platform components to build products for another manufacturer under their brand name. Value-added resellers incorporate platform software into their own software product packages. And managed service providers remotely monitor and install hardware and software platforms at the end customer's location, and may also provide software as a service on the cloud platform.

  独立软件供应商在平台供应商的合作伙伴计划中运行。此计划旨在涵盖一系列合作伙伴关系和互动，以利用联合优势，将其转化为平台软件更多的业务机会。ISV定制添加到其平台软件的专用软件，原始设备制造商使用组件以其品牌名称为其他制造商构建产品。增值经销商将平台软件整合到他们自己的软件产品包中。托管服务提供商可以远程监控和安装硬件和软件平台，还可以在云平台上提供软件服务给最终客户。

Indirect channels-Distribution Marketing Partners
间接渠道 - 分销营销合作伙伴

Affinity Marketing Partnership 相关营销伙伴关系

  This can be a modified form of distribution marketing partnership by introducing unique offers to the target group of consumers. These offers typically contain a package of products or services that align with the consumers' purchasing preferences.

  相关营销伙伴可以是通过合作形式向目标消费者群体提供独特优惠来促进分销营销。这些优惠通常包含符合消费者购买偏好的产品或服务。

  An easy example of this is when a cinema and a credit card company working together. The credit card company is looking forward to establishing a new customer base: particularly, cinema customer who never had a credit card before. So, they partner with a cinema operator to offer their specialized product, such as a credit card developed especially for cinema customer. The card would most likely be branded with the cinema's logo, and special incentives are offered to cinema customer when they use their credit card to pay for a movie ticket, food, and beverage at the cinema.

电影院和银行合作是一个很好的例子。银行可以建立一个新的客户群：特别针对未有过信用卡的电影客户。银行与电影院运营商合作提供的专属产品，例如专为电影客户开发的信用卡。信用卡有电影院的商标，当客户使用信用卡支付电影院的戏票，食品和饮料时，电影院和银行为客户提供特惠和其它奖励。

Affinity marketing partnerships allow the partner brands collaborating to offer unique discounts, services and/or products to target customers related to the partners' brands, as such they will have a high probability for purchasing the products of both partners.

相关营销合作伙伴关系允许合作伙伴品牌为目标客户提供与品牌相关的特惠,服务或产品,因此能够吸引彼此的客户购买这些专属产品。

Sponsorship Marketing Partnership 赞助营销合作伙伴

In a sponsorship marketing partnership, one partner advertises its brand on the other entity typically the media company, big sport event, charity events for publicity. For example, electrical company Hisense is the sponsor for FIFA world cup 2018.

在赞助营销合作伙伴关系中，合作伙伴在通常是媒体公司，大型体育赛事，宣传慈善活动的平台上宣传其品牌。例如，电气公司海信是2018年FIFA世界杯的赞助商。

Affiliate Marketing Partnership 联盟营销合作伙伴

The company with e-commerce business can reach more customers via the affiliate program. They may use their partner's network to tap into different customer segments. In most cases, affiliate marketing partners can help to expand sales beyond the geographical regions or customer segments.

拥有电子商务业务的公司可以通过联盟计划开拓更多客源。他们可能会使用其合作伙伴的网络来联系不同的客户群。在大多数情况下，联盟营销合作伙伴可以帮助扩大地理区域之外的客户群。

A partner who offers affiliate programs often gets commission or referral fee from its e-commerce partner on products sold and/or leads generated. To compensate for the commission cost, some companies choose to raise their offering price, while others maintain their price by absorbing the cost themselves. A lot of marketing and advertising companies offer affiliate programs; among the popular ones are Commission Junction, LinkShare, Rakuten.

提供联盟计划的合作伙伴通常会从其电子商务合作伙伴那里获得销售产品和的佣金或推荐费。为了弥补佣金成本，一些公司选择提高售价，而其他公司则通过自己承担成本来维持价格。许多营销和广告公司都提供联盟计划包括 Commission Junction, LinkShare, Rakuten.

Partner Relationship Management 伙伴关系管理

Channel conflicts often arise between channels that are perceived as counterproductive or unfair. For example, e-commerce business partner who undercuts the retail partners' profit. To reduce the pricing advantage of e-commerce channel, the vendor must allow a retail partner to have new items weeks before they are available on the e-commerce platform to compensate for the traditional retailer higher overhead expenses. Other than that, the vendor may also provide the training to build an e-commerce platform for a retailer to increase the sales via click and mortar approach.

渠道冲突经常发生在被认为适得其反或不公平的渠道之间。例如，电子商务业务合作伙伴削弱了零售合作伙伴的利润。为了降低电子商务渠道的价格优势，供应商必须允许零售合作伙伴在电子商务平台上架之前几周获得新产品，以弥补传统零售商更高的管理费用。除此之外，供应商还可以提供培训，为零售商建立电子商务平台，通过上下线模式增加销售额。

Channel conflict comes in many forms. For the less severe case, it is merely the necessary moves to maintain the competitiveness of the business environment. It is positive for the manufacturer to remain relevant in the market via forcing obsolete or uneconomic dealers to adapt or decline. Other severe conflicts, however, can be detrimental to the manufacturer's business model. These high-risk conflicts generally happen when there are overlapping customer segments already served by an existing channel causing the cannibalization of product. This causes the decline of channel economics that the threatened channel partner either stops selling the product or even selling the product of a competitor. An entrepreneur who crafting the channel strategy must strike a balance of both direct and indirect channels to avoid potential channel conflict.

渠道冲突有多种形式。对轻微的情况，这仅仅是维持商业环境竞争力的必要举措。通过迫使过时或不经济的经销商适应或退出销售，制造商可以顺应市场的需求。但是，其他严重的冲突可能对制造商的商业模式不利。这些高风险冲突通常发生在现有渠道已经服务重叠的客户群导致产品销售下滑。这导致渠道的经济效益下降，受威胁的渠道合作伙伴要么停止销售产品，要么销售竞争对手的产品。制定渠道战略的企业家必须在直接和间接渠道之间取得平衡，以避免潜在的渠道冲突。

Chapter 6- Revenues 第六章 - 收入

Revenues 收入

Revenue is the income generated from sale activity of goods and services. It often involves the transfer of ownership or access rights from the seller to the user when payment is made for the products or services. Revenue is typically shown as the top item (top line) in the profit and loss statement from which all other expenses are deducted to get net income (bottom line).

收入是商品和服务销售活动产生的收益。它通常涉及用户支付产品或服务费用时将所有权从用户转移到卖方。收入通常显示在损益表中的顶级项目，从中扣除所有其他费用以获得净收入。

Generally, there are seven main ways of creating revenue: asset sales, usage fees, subscription fees, lending/leasing/renting, licensing, brokerage fees, and advertising.

The entrepreneur may choose the appropriate revenue stream according to the business nature through the application of the value proposition framework (See Chapter 3).

有七种主要的收入来源：资产销售，使用费，签购费，贷款/租赁/租赁，许可证经营，经纪费和广告。企业家可以通过应用价值主张框架，根据业务性质选择合适的收入流（见第3章）。

Asset sale 资产销售

An asset sale is completed, when the buyer obtains the goods delivered by a company. Asset Sale – the most common type involves the sale of a current asset which is a part of the inventory. Selling ownership rights of tangible goods to consumers is quite normal for a retailer. For example, an asset sale occurs when a computer store delivers a Personal

Computer to a customer. By doing this, the customer owns a PC for personal use.

当买方获得公司交付的货物时，资产销售即告完成。资产出售 - 最常见的类型涉及出售作为库存一部分的流动资产。向消费者出售有形商品的所有权对零售商来说是很常见的。例如，当商店将个人计算机递送给客户就是资产销售。收货后，客户拥有一台个人使用的PC。

It is difficult to differentiate between companies according to whether they sell services or goods in the today competitive market. A more useful way to make the distinction is focusing on the *intangibles* and *tangibles*. Entrepreneur sells intangibles to consumers, no matter what is manufactured in the factory. While some of the dissimilarity might seem apparent, it is obvious that there are a lot of similarities between the marketing of intangibles and tangibles.

在当今竞争激烈的市场很难区分销售中的服务或商品。一种更有效的区分方法是关注无形资产和有形资产。无论工厂生产什么，企业家都会向消费者出售无形资产。虽服务或商品一些不相似的地方显而易见。但是，无形资产和有形资产的营销之间存在很多相似之处。

The key area of similarity in the marketing of intangibles and tangibles revolves around the intangibility. Marketing is often associated with getting new customers and keeping the existing customers. The degree of product intangibility has its greatest effect in both areas.

无形资产和有形资产营销相似的关键领域围绕着无形资产。营销通常与获得新客户和保持现有客户有关。产品无形性程度在这两处有最大的影响。

The intangibility of all products 产品的无形性

The intangibles can determine the product's success, even with mature consumer goods like shampoo, and frozen food. If it is not functioned as intended, for instance, a shampoo is not cleaned as advertised, or frozen food cannot be eaten as stated on the label, the results can be terrible. User can't experience in advance the moderate-to-low-priced goods such as canned foods or detergents. To convince buyers more comfortable with the tangibles that can't be tested, companies must go beyond the actual promises of specifications, using advertisements, and labels to provide reassurance of the products' utility.

无形资产可以决定产品的成功，即使是成熟的消费品，如洗发水和冷冻食品。例如，如果没有按照预期运作，洗发水不像所宣传的那样洗干净头发，或者冷冻食品不能像标签上所述那样食用，结果可能很糟糕。用户无法提前体验中等至低价商品，如罐头食品或洗涤剂。为了让买家更加了解无法测试的物品，公司必须超越实际的体验规格，利用广告和标签以提供产品效用的保证。

Packaging is one common tool to visualize the intangibility. For Instance, honey put into see-through glass jars, cookies into sealed-windowed boxes, canned goods get a strong appetizing photo and label on the surface of the packaging. In all cases, the main idea is to provide a reassuring effect on tangibility for what's promised but can't be directly delivered before the sale.

包装是可视化无形性的一种常用工具。例如，蜂蜜放入透明的玻璃罐中，饼干放入密封的窗口盒中，罐装食品在包装上印有开胃照片和标签。在这样情况下，主要是提供令消费人保证，在销售前让他们了解产品的效用。

Common sense shows us, and the academic study indicates that people use the appearances to make judgments of their real world. It does not matter whether the product is expensive or cheap, whether the product is complex or easy to use, whether the buyers are tech savvy or ignorant, or whether they buy for themselves or others. Everybody relies on both physical appearances and impressions to make a purchase decision.

常识告诉我们，学术研究表明人们利用外表来判断他们的现实世界。无论产品是昂贵还是便宜，产品是否复杂或易于使用，或者是为自己还是其他人购买都无关紧要。每个人都依赖于外表和印象来做出购买决定。

The product will be gauged in two major parts—not by just which the company is but also the people who represent it. The company and its people are both parts of the "product" that customers must consider before they buy. The less tangible the product, the more powerfully and persistently the judgment about it gets shaped by the packaging—how it's displayed, who presents it, and what's implied by metaphor, symbol, and other replacement for the tangibility of the product.

产品将分为两个主要部分－不仅仅是公司而已，而是代表它的人。公司及其员工都是客户购买前必须考虑的"产品"的一部分。产品越无形，消费者对它的判断就越容易被包装塑造。包装的展示，呈现，以及隐喻，符号可替代产品的有形性。

The way the product is presented in the sales process (how it is shown in the brochure, letter, design appearance), how it is presented by people, and by whom—all these become critical components of the product and influence the customer purchase intention.

产品在销售过程中的呈现方式（在小册子，信函，设计外观），公司的代表如何呈现产品 - 这些都成为影响客户购买产品的关键因素。

Service Revenue 服务收入

Service Revenue refers to income earned from providing intangible products or services such as technical services, consulting or other specialist services as a part of the trade, profession or business. It is the main source of income for service-oriented businesses. It could take the form of monthly bills or even a commercial contract. For example, a monthly mobile phone contract, unless the contract is terminated or the customers do not pay on time, the service providers can gain the recurring sales for the agreed period.

服务收入是提供技术服务，咨询或其他专业服务等无形产品或服务所赚取的收入。它是服务型企业的主要收入来源。它可以采取月度账单甚至商业合同的形式。例如，每月移动电话合同，除非合同终止或客户未按时付款，服务提供商可以在指定的时间内获得定期销售。

You may offer a service at a low introductory price or even freemium to grow your customer base and as lead generation tool for the other more expensive services. Lastly, provide a service that leverage on your experiences, skillsets, and the things that you are good at. You may need to figure out what you're good at and find an appealing way to sell it repeatedly.

您可以以较低的入门价格提供服务，甚至免费增值服务以扩大您的客户群，并作为其他更昂贵服务的潜在客户生成工具。提供一种利用您的经验，技能组合以及您擅长的事物的服务。您可能需要弄清楚自己擅长什么，并找到一种吸引消费人的方式来反复出售它。

Subscription 签购

Subscription-A company sells the repeated access to a product or a service. For Instance, Telco companies generally sell a phone bundled with data and talk plan through a monthly subscription. Subscription business model was pioneered by traditional media such as magazines and newspapers. This model is enticing because a contract binds the user to pay consistently for the product or service. It means that a company can make much more recurring revenue.

 签购 - 公司出售对产品或服务的重复使用权。电信公司通常通过每月签购配套中捆绑了数据和通话时间。订阅商业模式是由杂志和报纸等传统媒体开创的。这种模式很诱人，因为合同会约束用户对产品或服务的支付费用。这意味着公司可以获得更多的经常性收入。

 The entrepreneurs may sell one-off basis or periodic access of services to the customer. For instance, a theatre sells the subscription pass as the package deal to the customer. A one-time sale of the pass turns into a recurring sale that builds brand loyalty. The user is tracked in both a subscribed and unsubscribed status within the business to grow member base over time.

企业家可以一次性出售或定期向客户提供服务。例如，剧院将签购通行证作为配套出售给顾客。一次性出售通票变成了经常性的销售，也同时建立了品牌忠诚度。以订阅和未订阅来区分用户，从中建立新的客户群。

Membership of a certain type of organizations or any other special interest groups are also known as subscriptions. For instance book clubs, music clubs, cable television, satellite television, satellite radio, mobile network operators, internet providers, software, websites (e.g., blogging websites), business solutions providers, financial services firms, health clubs, as well as the media such as newspapers, magazines, and academic journals. Renewal of a subscription may be activated by period selectively or activated automatically, the payment can be settled by a pre-authorized credit card or via bank account.

组织或任何其他特殊兴趣组织的成员也常用订阅模式。例如书籍俱乐部，音乐俱乐部，有线电视，卫星电视，卫星广播，移动网络运营商，互联网提供商，软件，网站（例如博客网站），商业解决方案提供商，金融服务公司，健康俱乐部以及媒体如报纸，杂志和学术期刊。订阅的更新可以通过选择性地自动更新，可通过预授权的信用卡或通过银行账户来支付费用。

For a web-based application, the freemium model is common by providing the basic features for free access, but restrict access of premium features to the free users. It can be applied to both unlimited and periodic access. For unrestricted access, an entrepreneur must ensure the availability and consistency of the subscribed features. For periodic access, the web-based application must be updated from in terms of contents, features and providing continuous support for user consistently to retain them. At the same time, it helps to generate recurring revenues for the company.

对于线上的应用程序，免费增值模式通常是提供免费使用基本功能，但限制用户使用高端功能。它可以应用于无限制和定期使用者。对于不受限制的使用，企业家必须确保订阅功能的可用性和一致性。对于定期使用者，必须从内容，功能方面更新网络的应用程序，并始终为用户提供支援服务以保留他们成为长期客户。同时，它有助于为公司产生经常性收入。

In terms of circulation of the subscription, an entrepreneur can control the circulation of the subscription to increase the revenue by a number of devices for a subscription. For instance, Microsoft office 365 basic plan is now limited to 365 days for five devices. For unlimited access, Microsoft office software limits one license for each device.

在订阅的流通方面，企业家可以控制订阅的流通以增加用于订阅的多个设备的收入。例如，对于五台设备，Microsoft Office 365 基本计划现在限制为 365 天。对于无限制使用，Microsoft Office 软件限制每个许可证只可用在一台设备。

Lending 借贷

The private lending business model is more viable when you focus locally. Most of your loans should come from within the city or even from the local community. Determine the funding capacity of your investor. If it is between $1 000 to $100 000, then set this as the niche market. Other than that, if your clients need the fund of $1000, provide the same amount loan with an attractive interest rate with fast approval, minimum paperwork for them to get the money instantly.

当您专注于区域的业务，私人借贷业务模式可行性可以大大地提升。您的大部分贷款应来自同一个城市，甚至来自社区的客户。确定投资者的融资能力。如果它在1 000元到10万元之间，那么将其定为利基市场。除此之外，如果您的客户需要1000美元的资金，提供相同金额的贷款，确保低利率和快速批准，最低限度的批文，以便他们立即获得资金。

Build business gradually with a small loan, creating more volume than offering a larger loan. You can create more earnings by doing the transactions of the microloan. As the big loan client often has higher bargaining power and requires a lower interest rate, causing the drop of interest earnings. If you focus on more transactions with clients with good payback records, you actually diversifying the risk and minimize the probability of default loan.

通过小额贷款逐步建立业务，创造更多的交易量而不是提供更大的贷款。您可以通过进行小额贷款的交易来创造更多收益。由于大额贷款客户往往具有较高的议价能力并降低的利率的收入，导致利息收益下降。如果您专注于与具有良好付款记录的客户进行更多交易，您实际上会使风险分散并最大限度地降低违约贷款的可能性。

  Be specific in advertising and marketing with the local community of the type of loan and the loan amounts. Build the trustworthiness of your business within the community, design a website with photos and testimonials on actual deals your company has funded. Show the testimonials with your names, addresses, pictures, and email addresses for all clients to see it on the website. Use the phone number and postcode to show your locality attracting nearby clients. Attend industry seminars and seek advice from those who have succeeded in the business. Hire an industry expert to review your business practices and legal compliance with state and federal regulations. Conduct this business with integrity, and soon you will have a steady base of customers with the reputation build within the community.

贷款和贷款金额的广告和营销需要针对服务社区客户的需求。在社区内建立您的企业的声誉，设计一个网站，其中包含您公司资助的实际交易的照片和贷款人的推荐。显示您的姓名，地址，图片和电子邮件地址，以便所有客户在网站上查看。使用电话号码和邮政编码显示所在地吸引附近客户。参加行业研讨会，并寻求务成功业者的建议。聘请行业专家来审查您的业务以及遵守州和联邦法规的法律合规性。诚信经营这项业务，很快您将拥有稳定的客户群，并在社区内建立声誉。

Renting 出租

Renting has long been a well-known moneymaking business because most people can't afford to purchase a high-value asset. However, they can afford to spend a small amount of money to gain access. Typical rental businesses include tools, watercraft, construction equipment, recreational vehicles, lodgings, musical instruments, office furniture and equipment, canoes and kayaks, camping equipment.

出租一直是众所周知的赚钱业务，因为大多数人买不起高价值资产。但是，他们可以花费少量资金来获取使用权。典型的出租业务包括工具，船只，建筑设备，休闲车，住宿，乐器，办公家具和设备，独木舟和皮划艇，野营装备。

Start-up costs can be substantial depending on the asset you purchase to rent. However, you can reduce costs by purchasing used assets in good condition. Alternatively, you may even gather the owners of the assets to establish a rental pool, keeping a portion of the management fees for providing the services. Avoid idle inventory at all costs–it only occupies storage space and cash flow you could use to grow your business! Don't overspend on equipment initially: buy your minimum viable inventory based on your market research. Instead of buying the asset with cash, purchase it using the available financing scheme. Once your business gets bigger, buy the equipment that is more popular, lucrative based on customer preference. It is cheaper and easier to buy more equipment later than to get rid of excess and obsolete asset/equipment.

　　出租资产的成本可能很高。但是，您可以通过购买状况良好的旧资产来降低成本。或者，您甚至可以集合资产的所有者以建立出租服务，保留一部分管理费为收入。避免闲置库存 - 它只占用您可用来发展业务的存储空间和现金流量！最初不要购入过于奢华的设备或资产：根据您的市场调查购买有需求的资产。不用现金购买资产，而是使用融资方案购买。一旦您的业务提升时，根据客户的喜好购买更受欢迎，利润丰厚的资产。在业务成长时购买更多合适的设备比报销多余和过时的资产/设备更便宜，容易。

Starting the similar business in two locations can lead to distinct business requirements. A car rental in the city will have different customers than one in the suburban area. So, make sure you know the target customers' need. Other than that, you may offer extra service related to your business. Contact the related businesses for referral partnership. Find partners with quality products and services to ensure the customer satisfaction for recurring sales. For instance, car rental customers might need the service of the eatery, data roaming, accommodation, a ticket to a tourist spot, activities of interest, etc. By referring customers to each other business. You create a win-win situation that both parties get more customers. Your customers get the one-stop solution and easy access to services and products they need.

在两个地点开始类似的业务会有不同的业务需求。城市的汽车出租客户不同于郊区的客户的需求。因此，请确保您了解目标客户的需求。除此之外，您可以提供与您的业务相关的额外服务。联系相关企业以推荐合作伙伴的业务。寻找提供优质产品和服务的合作伙伴，以确保客户满意和留住客户。例如，汽车出租客户可能需要餐馆的服务，数据漫游，住宿，旅游景点的门票，活动等。通过向客户介绍的合作伙伴的业务。您创造了一个双赢的局面，双方都能获得更多客户。您的客户可以获得一站式解决方案，并轻松获得所需的服务和产品。

So, while you want to make sure you have good insurance coverage for the rental assets. The customers are your largest risk too. Even with no-liability waivers, make sure you cover the rental services with the right insurance to protect the customer. In the event of unforeseen circumstances, the insurance claims may provide necessary compensation without using a large sum of your company's cash.

确保您拥有良好的资产保险。客户也是您最大的风险。即使没有免责声明，也请务必使用适当的保险来保障租赁服务和保护客户。在突发情况下，保险索赔可以提供必要的补偿，而无需使用公司的大笔现金。

For the asset maintenance, you may schedule regular preventive maintenance to prevent the future breakdown. It is important for the quality and safety of the rental service. In case of the sudden breakdown, fix any issues promptly and completely with your own maintenance team or outsourced professionals. Cosmetic maintenance is important for the appeal of your rental asset, make sure your assets look like new to create a nice impression to potential customers.

对于资产维护，您可以安排定期预防性维护，以防止将来发生故障。这对于租赁服务的质量和安全非常重要。如果突然发生故障，请立即与您自己的维护团队或外包专业人员及时解决问题。外部维护对于您的租赁资产的吸引力非常重要，确保资产看起来像新的一样，以便为潜在客户创造良好的印象。

Rental agreements are an important document to clarify the terms and conditions like the specification of the asset, duration, fee, security deposits, insurance indemnification, and penalty term. You need to communicate terms and conditions to the customer before handling over the asset to them. Customers often need to sign the hard copy or website agreement. It is an important document to protect the mutual interest of both parties.

租赁协议是说明条款和条件的重要文件，如资产说明，期限，费用，保证金，保险赔偿和罚款期限。在将资产交给客户之前，您需要向客户解释条款和条件。客户经常需要签署租约或网上协议。这是保护双方共同利益的重要文件。

Make sure you create a good impression to potential customers. Rentals are recurring business–most customers only use the asset for a short period, so if they need to use the asset later, they have to rent again. Make sure that when they need the service, they become your repeat customers! Create a unique proposition to make your customers feel welcome and give them one-stop solution service with friendly customer support. Create a hassle-free experience–don't frustrate your customers with tons of paperwork and procedures. If you've followed all of this advice, you already have a nice overall idea by now, about what you should do to create a successful rental business.

确保您为潜在客户留下良好印象。出租是长期性的业务 - 大多数客户只在短期内使用该资产，因此如果他们以后需要使用该资产，他们必须再次租用。确保在他们需要服务时，他们成为您的回头客！创建一个独特的价值，让您的客户感到宾至如归，并通过友好的客户支持为他们提供一站式解决方案服务。创造无忧无虑的体验 - 不要因为大量的批文和程序而使您的客户感到沮丧。如果您已经遵循了这些建议，那么您现在已经有了一个很好的概念，如何创建一个成功的出租业务。

Leasing 租赁

Leasing business model typically involves three main parties, i.e. the seller, the buyer and financier /bank. The seller contracts with the buyer of the periodic fees during the tenure. At the end of the payment, the seller may reclaim the ownership or transfer it to the buyer. Leasing business is common in transactions involving the exchange of expensive assets such as the medical device and industrial equipment. There are the two main markets for the leasing of equipment. "Big-ticket items" such as heavy machinery, commercial vehicles, diagnostic equipment and devices, manufacturing equipment, and physical infrastructure like commercial property, solar power systems are typical examples of items that may generate income through leasing arrangements.

租赁业务模式通常涉及三个主要方，即卖方，买方和融资方/银行。在租期内，卖方与买方签订定期费用。在付款结束时，卖方可以收回所有权或将其转让给买方。租赁业务在涉及昂贵资产（如医疗设备和工业设备）的交易中很常见。租赁主要市场如：重型机械，商用车辆，诊断设备和装置，制造设备以及商业地产，基础设施的昂贵资产是可通过租赁产生收入的的典型例子。

  Because of the long leasing period, leasing arrangements require the collaborative relationships between sellers and lessors. Quality control is important in leasing arrangements since it requires the asset to perform consistently. Often a service agreement drafted requiring the seller to provide technical support and service maintenance throughout the term of the contract. Because contracts extend over a long duration, recurring sales from the same customer is an important source of income. Thus, sellers of leased equipment rely heavily on relationship-building with customer service and after-sales-service to gain trust from customers. Operating with leasing revenue requires sales personnel to focus on generating repeat sales in the form of lease renewals or extended period of leasing arrangements. The cost of financing is another important success factor, leasing business requires the participation of a financial institution for funding since it is capital intensive.

　　由于租赁期较长，租赁安排需要卖方与出租人之间的协作关系。质量控制在租赁中很重要，因为租赁资产需要长期的运行。在服务协议中，卖方会在整个合同期限内提供技术支持和服务维护。由于合同期限较长，因此同一客户的经常性销售是重要的收入来源。因此，租赁设备的销售商在很大程度上依赖于与客户服务和售后服务的关系建立来获得客户的信任。以租赁收入运营需要销售人员专注于以续租或延长租赁的形式产生重复销售。融资成本是另一个重要的成功因素，租赁业务需要金融机构的参与，因为租赁是资本密集型的商业模式。

Leasing agreement is often complex. All stakeholders need to understand the contract to prevent confusion and dispute. Leasing is a great business model for expanding the market for expensive items to customers who lack a large sum of cash or prefer financing. Besides that, leasing is a viable business model in most high-value items, since it absorbs the high processing cost and operational expenses gradually via financing.

租赁协议通常很复杂。所有利益相关者都需要了解合同以防止争议。租赁是一种很好的商业模式，它可以将昂贵物品的市场扩展到缺乏大量现金或喜欢融资的客户。除此之外，租赁是大多数高价值物品的可行商业模式，因为它通过融资逐渐吸纳高昂的加工成本和运营费用。

Broker 经纪人

The entrepreneur may generate income via intermediation service as the broker via an online or offline service. Brokers are market-makers: They facilitate transactions between buyers and sellers. Brokers play a major role in consumer-to-consumer (C2C), business-to-business (B2B), business-to-consumer (B2C) business. Typically, brokers charge a nominal fee or commission for each transaction fulfill in the market. They can charge the commission at a different rate from one industry to another. Brokerage fees are income created from an intermediary service via the order fulfillment between buyer and seller. For example, a property agent gains commission based on a percentage of property value.

企业家可以通过中介服务作为经纪人通过在线或离线服务产生收入。经纪人是做市商：他们促进买卖双方之间的交易。经纪人在消费者对消费者（C2C），企业对企业（B2B），企业对消费者（B2C）业务中发挥着重要作用。通常，经纪人为市场中的每笔交易收指定的费用或佣金。他们可以从一个行业到另一个行业以不同的费率收取佣金。经纪费是指通过买方和卖方之间的订单履行从中介服务创建的收入。例如，房地产经纪人根据房产价值的百分比获得佣金。

  Marketplace brokers are agents who provide a full range of services. Their service ranges from advisory service, market assessment to negotiation and fulfillment, for a particular industry. The marketplace can operate by a company, or an industry consortium with the big players in the industry. For example, an insurance agent works for a particular insurance company; an insurance broker may work for different insurance companies.

市场经纪人是提供全方位服务的代理商。他们的服务范围从咨询服务，市场评估到谈判和履行，适用于特定行业。市场可以由公司或行业联盟与业内的大公司共同运营。例如，保险代理人为特定的保险公司工作；保险经纪人可以为不同的保险公司工作。

Demand collection system is the business model pioneered by Priceline in which the users can advertise their demand with the desired price to a group of sellers online. Then. Priceline will try to match the demand with the interested sellers who provide the desired price offering by the user. The company will gain the commission via the fulfilled transaction online. Distributor — is an intermediary operation that connects many product manufacturers with volume and retail buyers. A broker facilitates business transactions between franchised distributors and their trading partners.

　　需求收集系统是Priceline开创的商业模式，其中用户可以在线向一组卖家以期望的价格展示他们的需求。然后。Priceline将尝试将用户所提供价格与卖家的售价互相匹配。公司将通过在线完成的交易获得佣金。分销商 - 是一个中间业务，将许多产品制造商与批量和零售买家联系起来。经纪人也可促进特许经销商与其贸易伙伴之间的商业交易。

Auction broker conducts auctions for either individuals or merchants to get the highest bidder in the market. Reverse auctions are a common variant which the buyer sourcing items via contact to get the lowest price seller in the market. Reverse auction helps the buyer to decrease the price; as the sellers compete to offer the best price or deal whilst meeting the expectation stated in the contract. Auction broker charges the seller a listing fee according to the value of the transaction.

　　拍卖经纪人为个人或商家进行拍卖，以获得市场上最高买家。反向拍卖是买方通过联系卖方采购物品以获得市场上最低价格。反向拍卖有助于买方降低价格；因为卖方的竞争买方可以获得最优惠的价格或交易，同时满足合同中规定的条款。拍卖经纪人根据交易价格向卖方收取佣金。

　　Transaction broker provides a third-party payment mechanism via an online platform for buyers and sellers to facilitate a transaction. For instance, fsbohouse.com offers an online platform for sellers or buyers to facilitate the property deal with lower commission than traditional real estate agents. Distributor network with many product manufacturers and retail buyers often need the broker to make the deal between them. For instance, the broker facilitates business transactions between franchised distributors and their trading partners.

交易经纪人通过在线平台为买卖双方提供第三方支付机制，以促进交易。例如，fsbohouse.com 为卖家或买家提供了一个在线平台，以促进与传统房地产经纪人相比较低佣金的房产交易。与许多产品制造商和零售买家的经销商网络经常需要经纪人在他们之间进行交易。例如，经纪人促进特许经销商与其贸易伙伴之间的商业交易。

Bounty broker is given a prize for searching the difficult to find item, person, idea. Search agent performs the searching activity for information such as the price and availability for a good or service specified by the buyer. Web crawlers also known as spiders, crawlers, are programs that browse through the Internet using an algorithm to index content systematically. The market for web crawling service is mainly driven by the growing demand for business intelligence. It provides collective information, and the general market trends enable organizations to gain a competitive edge over competitors. All search brokers often reward with a flat fee or a percentage of rewards from the found items.

赏金经纪人获得了搜索难以找到的项目，人物，想法的奖励。搜索代理执行搜索活动，以获取买方指定的商品或服务的价格和可用性等信息。 网络爬虫（也称为蜘蛛，爬虫）是使用算法系统地索引内容来浏览 Internet 的程序。网络爬行服务市场主要受商业智能需求的增长推动。它提供集体信息，一般市场趋势使组织能够获得竞争优势。所有搜索经纪人通常会从找到的项目中获得固定费用或一定比例的奖励。

Licensing 许可证贸易

Licensing content, product, technology can be a great source of revenue for a startup business. This may be done either by charging the licensors (users) for a flat or variable fee. Charging a fee on the licensed product is common in non-competitive business line, and for the non-sales purpose. Here, the licensor is an end user. Therefore, it is more reasonable to charge the licensor with either a fixed or used fee. If your licensor is in the same line of business and uses the products for sales, then charging a percentage of the revenue is a better approach. This way, the licensee (owner) makes recurring revenues each time their licensed product is sold by a licensor.

　　许可内容，产品，技术可以成为企业的重要收入来源。这可以通过向许可人（用户）收取固定费用或可变费用。对许可产品收取费用在非竞争性业务线中是常见的，并且用于非销售目的。在这模式里，许可人是最终用户。因此，向许可人收取固定费用或使用费是更合理的。如果您的许可人处于同一业务范围并将产品用于销售,那么收取一定比例的收入是一种更好的方法。这样,被许可人(所有者)每次出售其许可产品时就能产生经常性的收入。

Licensing is money-making, especially in software development and content creation business. Identifying the right revenue model, and picking the target segment of the customer is important in establishing a sustainable business model.

许可贸易是赚钱的,特别是在软件开发和内容创建业务中。确定正确的收入模型,并选择锁定的目标客户对于建立可持续的业务模式至关重要。

Licensing provides the opportunity for businesses to expand without using their own resources by venturing into non-related industry business. Licensee may collaborate with another industry partner to build sophisticated products and services. For instance, Google offers its Google map service with Uber to develop a navigation system for the ride-hailing application.

　　许可证的使用让企业进入非相关行业业务，为企业无需使用自己的资源获得扩展业务的机会，被许可方可以与其他行业合作伙伴合作，以构建复杂的产品和服务。例如，谷歌为优步提供谷歌地图服务，为驾驶应用程序开发导航系统。

Licensing is not ideal for every business and could be detrimental if not deployed strategically. A general rule of thumb is not to license the direct competitor. Licensing would let a weaker rival offers a product as well as yours, or a stronger competitor to overcome the shortcoming. The ideal licensing model is where your product forms a vital component, for the non-competitor in a different industry. Uber leveraging on Google Maps is the mutual benefit example of a licensing model. Other common licensing models, including music for use in an event, commercial space, theatre, movie and the patents in the electronic devices. For instance, Google and Android phone manufacturer have cross-licensing agreements to utilize each other's patents in a non- competitive position to create a more customer-centric mobile device.

　　许可证贸易不是每个企业的理想模式，如果不进行战略部署，则可能是有害的。不与直接竞争对手进行许可贸易是其中一个方法。许可证贸易将让一个较弱的竞争对手提供产品以及您一样素质的产品，或更强大的竞争对手来克服本身产品的缺点。理想的许可模式是您的产品为不同行业的非竞争对手组成重要业务部分。优步利用谷歌地图是许可模式的互惠范例。其它常见的许可模式，包括用于活动的音乐，商业空间，剧院，电影和电子设备中的专利。例如，谷歌和Android手机制造商签订了交叉许可协议，以便在非竞争地位利用彼此的专利，从而创建更加以客户为中心的移动设备。

Advertising 广告

An advertising revenue model is a business approach that focuses on advertising as a major source of income. This revenue model is important in traditional broadcast, print media and modern online media. Media company gains income from advertising, customer subscriptions or both.

广告收入模式是一种将广告作为主要收入来源的商业方法。这种收入模式在传统广播，印刷媒体和现代在线媒体中常见。媒体公司通过广告，客户订阅或两者获得收入。

Traditional media like TV, radio, along with newspapers and magazines entertain or inform audiences or readers. TV and radio have traditionally been mainly advertising-supported. While networks and satellite TV stations earn part of revenue via viewer subscriptions, they earn most of their revenue from advertisers trying to appeal against the audiences. Similarly, magazines and newspapers charge subscription or purchase fees, but advertisers also pay to place ads within these print media. Modern entrepreneurs should focus on online media for the advertising revenue model.

电视，广播等传统媒体以及报纸和杂志为观众或读者提供娱乐或信息。电视和广播主要是传统上是以广告为主收入的。虽然网络和卫星电视台通过观众订阅获得部分收入，但他们的大部分收入来自试图向观众提出销售讯息的广告商。同样，杂志和报纸收取订阅或购买费用，但广告商也会付费在这些印刷媒体中放置广告。现代企业家应该关注于在线媒体广告收入模式。

The emergence of the Internet in the mid-1990s has disrupted the advertising revenue model. Newspaper's publisher, for instance, tried to shift for online content and reduced publication of hard copy. Modern media companies have established thousands of media websites, which offer free content for users. With the large user base, they attract businesses to advertise banner ads and advertorial ad spaces on their website. Traditional newspapers have shifted online with free content, but many are trying to figure out how to combine ad revenue with subscription fees.

20世纪90年代中期互联网的出现颠覆了广告收入模式。例如，报纸的出版商试图转移在线内容并减少纸上出版。现代媒体公司建立了媒体网站，为用户提供免费内容。凭借庞大的用户群，他们吸引企业在其网站上打广告。传统报纸已经通过免费内容转移到网上，但许多业者正试图将广告收入与订阅费相互结合。

The advantage of an advertising revenue model is that if you have a large base of viewers or subscribers, you can easily find companies that want to pay for advertisement. The ad-supported model is workable when you can provide the details of the niche of audiences to the businesses. When you operate on the ad-supported model without the subscription, you can easily attract users with free content. Both traditional and online media have long given away free content to the mass or target viewers, to drive up their reputation by increasing the circulation of free content, and subsequently the ramp up advertising revenue.

广告收入模式的优势在于拥有大量的观众或订阅者，这样可以轻松找到想要支付广告费用的公司。当您可以向企业提供受用户群体的详细信息，广告模式是可行的。这样您在没有订阅收入的广告的模式，可以轻松吸引免费内容的用户。传统媒体和在线媒体都长期向大众或目标观众赠送免费内容，通过增加免费内容的发行量来提高其声誉，并有效地提高广告收入。

The major disadvantage of 100% advertising revenue model is the inherent lack of diversification of income. During the economic downturn, most advertisers might cut their budgets on the advertisement, which reduce the revenue of the advertisers without subscription revenue. Besides that, costs on the website, publication and other overhead expenses are big of sustaining the business operation. Thus, a mixture of free and paid content can help to cover costs and entice viewers. The subscription revenue might not be substantial, but it helps offset costs and allow advertising revenue to build.

100%广告收入模式的主要缺点是缺乏多元化的收入。在经济衰退期间，大多数商家可能会削减广告预算，这会降低没有任何订阅模式的广告商收入。除此之外，网站上的成本，出版物和其他间接费用对维持业务运营至关重要。因此，免费和付费内容的混合可以帮助支付成本并吸引观众。订阅收入可能不大，但它有助于抵消部分成本并允许建立广告收入。

Revenue Management 收入管理

    The revenue management process begins with the data collection to create a model with a forecasting power. With the forecasting tool, entrepreneurs can derive the actionable insights from the data. They must also analyze the inventories, sales, prices, the volume of sales, customer information and other relevant data for market segmentation. It is used for market-based pricing and revenue maximization. For instance, Airlines charge differently for both business and economy class passengers, off-peak and peak season passengers, and different pricing via multiple channels such as online platform, travel agencies, and other ticket agents.

　　收益管理流程从数据收集开始，以创建具有预测能力的模型。利用预测工具，企业家可以从数据中获得可操作的见解。他们还必须分析库存，销售，价格，销售量，客户信息和其他相关数据以进行市场细分。它用于基于市场的定价和收入最大化。例如，航空公司对商务舱和经济舱乘客，非高峰和旺季乘客的收费不同，并通过多种渠道（如在线平台，旅行社和其他票务代理商）进行不同的定价。

Revenue management requires accurate forecasting on demand, price, and inventory. The revenue depends critically on the quality and accuracy of these forecasts. Thus, it is necessary to allocate resources and time to develop the right model with forecasting capabilities. Both Qualitative and Quantitative methods often complement each other shortcomings in forecasting. The qualitative method allows one to use the judgment and subjective knowledge in forecasting. One can make good use of a qualitative method, especially when there is no historical data for the new product. The Quantitative model depends on previous data and tries to model a scenario based on the variables in the data set. An entrepreneur can do policy making using a predictive model such as machine learning application. It explains past behavior well, but forecasting is only accurate as long as the existing collected data (independent variables) can explain the real-life condition of the market to give correct prediction (dependent variable).

收入管理需要对需求，价格和库存进行准确预测。收入主要取决于这些预测的质量和准确性。因此，有必要分配资源和时间来开发具有预测能力的正确模型。定性和定量方法通常在预测方面相互补充。定性方法允许人们在预测中使用判断和主观知识。人们可以很好地利用定性方法，特别是当没有新产品的历史数据时。定量模型依赖于先前的数据，并尝试基于数据集中的变量对场景进行建模。企业家可以使用预测模型（如机器学习应用程序）进行策略制定。它很好地解释了过去的行为，但只要现有的收集数据（自变量）可以解释市场的现实条件以给出正确的预测（因变量），预测就是相对准确的。

4 ways to increase revenues 4 种增加收入的方法

Acquiring the new customer 获取新客户

　　Acquiring the new customers means you're trying to bring more customers to your business. This is the most effective approach: as the number of customers grew, more patronage to business will generate more sales. You may need to segment, target and position your customers based on their lifestyles, buying habit to provide a solution of their concern issues. As customer habits are changing constantly, you should be reviewing the user profiles consistently, to ensure your business can detect any new trends from consumer purchase record.

获得新客户意味着您正在努力为您的企业带来更多客户。这是最有效的方法：随着客户数量的增长，对业务的更多赞助将产生更多的销售。您可能需要根据客户的生活方式细分，定位和定位客户，购买习惯以提供他们关注问题的解决方案。由于客户习惯不断变化，您应该常规地检查用户资料，以确保您的企业能够从消费者购买记录中检测到任何新趋势。

There are a number of non-competitive complementary businesses. These related businesses have broad customer bases of whom may also be the ideal customers for your company. By connecting and building mutually benefits partnership via referrals program, you greatly expanding customer base and creating another reliable source of income, to complement with existing sales channel.

有许多非竞争性的互补业务。这些相关业务拥有广泛的客户群，也可能是贵公司的理想客户。通过推荐计划连接和建立互惠伙伴关系，您可以大大扩展客户群并创造另一个可靠的收入来源，以补充现有的销售渠道。

Customers like special promotion or deal because it makes them feel like they're getting in on something worth more than the actual value. It also creates a sense of urgency, customers tend to purchase the promotional items as quickly as possible before the end of sales. The most rewarding sales campaigns don't just capture the attention of the customers, but they inspire it sharing as well. Social media channels are an ideal channel for free advertising, building the brand and reputation online. When users share your sales campaign, their immediate family and friends are more likely to be influenced. Because it's coming from someone they familiar, and trust to have their best interest in mind, rather than an advertisement from an unknown company.

客户喜欢特别促销或交易，因为这让他们觉得他们可以拥有价钱超过实际价值的东西。促销还会产生紧迫感，客户倾向于在销售结束前尽快购买促销品。最有价值的销售活动不仅吸引了客户的注意力，而且还激发了它的共享。社交媒体是在线建立品牌，声誉的理想渠道和免费广告。当用户分享您的销售活动时，他们的直系亲属和朋友更有可能受到影响。因为它来自他们熟悉并且信任的人，而不只是来自公司的广告。

A commercial website is another important tool for a business to get new customers. A website contains free, useful information on products or services for visitors. Besides that, it's imperative that the website comes with dedicated lead generation pages. Other than that, it must get the contact information and sales conversion page. These can be content pages that customers connect to via email, promotion webpage, or marketing campaigns. Be sure that they have free giveaways, click to action (CTA) buttons, consultation forms, or whatever method to get customers' information. Customer testimonials, reviews, and recommendations are some of the most powerful tools to entice online customers. Customers don't actually connect directly with a company; they connect with the people that associate with it. Give your customers the freedom to comment on your website, to remind they aren't just buying a "product," they are buying the access to a community of like-minded people whom they can interact with each other. Any form of positive social proof can increase the conversion rate. It addressing some of the doubt that may be holding the potential customers back, as they tend to make purchase decisions influenced by favorable comments from the existing customers.

商业网站是企业获得新客户的另一个重要工具。网站包含有关产品或服务的免费有用信息。除此之外，网站必须提供专用的潜在客户生成页面。除此之外，它必须获取联系信息和销售转换页面。这些可以是客户通过电子邮件，促销网页或营销活动连接到的内容页面。确保他们有免费赠品，点击操作（CTA）按钮，咨询表格或任何方法来获取客户的信息。客户的评论和推荐是吸引在线客户的最有力工具。客户实际上并不直接与公司联系；他们与公司相关的人联系。让您的客户可以自由评论您的网站，提醒他们不仅仅是购买"产品"，而是购买他们可以互相交流的志同道合者社区平台。任何形式的社交好评可以提高转换率。它减少了可能阻碍潜在客户购买的一些疑问，使他们倾向于受到现有客户的好评做出购买决策。

Retaining existing customer 留住现有客户

Keeping the existing customer means encouraging existing customers to purchase from you more often. For example, if your customers purchase once a month, convincing them to buy once a week will increase sales significantly. The more frequently they purchase, the higher income your business will bring in, assuming the average transaction value stays the same.

保持现有客户意味着鼓励现有客户更频繁地向您购买。例如，如果您的客户每月购买一次，说服他们每周购买一次将大大增加销售额。假设平均交易价值保持不变，他们购买的频率越高，您的业务收入就越高。

The good customer relationship is the best way to keep existing customers. Reward them with exclusive benefits as an appreciation for their patronage. For instance, as customers order their fourth product from your company. A week later, they receive a free cash voucher with a handwritten note thanking them for the purchase. This type of unexpected appreciation helps to improve overall customer satisfaction and offsetting the tiny cost of gifts. Genuinely care about your customers! It doesn't mean doing superficial things like sending little gifts, smiling at your meetings, but doing a study to learn more about new technologies or options that might benefit them in the long run. Be proactive to customers' needs, and responsive in gathering and engaging with the feedback is important to keep them happy.

良好的客户关系是留住现有客户的最佳方式。以独家的优惠奖励客户，以感谢他们的光顾。例如，当客户从贵公司订购他们的第四个产品时。一周后，他们收到一张带有手写便条的免费现金券，感谢他们购买。这种意想不到优惠的有助于提高整体客户满意度并抵消礼品的微小成本。真正关心您的客户！这并不意味着做一些肤浅的事情，比如发送小礼物，微笑面对顾客，而是做一项研究，以了解更多有关长期可能使他们受益的产品或服务。积极主动地满足客户的需求，积极收集意见和反馈让他们满意是至关重要的。

Using the data of purchased history or browsed record on the website, entrepreneurs can design the specific content and product recommendations in marketing campaigns. They may test incentives (discount, promotion) and other non-incentive factors (content of marketing material) to create the most effective way enticing the repeat customer. Top eCommerce company often emphasize the limited-time promotion. The visitors must complete the purchase quickly to get the special deal. In addition, you can add the coupon, gift card to the shopper's cart automatically, and highlight the deal during the checkout process. This promotion kills two birds with one stone: the limited-time deal increases the conversion rate in the most recent period, and the gift card brings customers back to the website to make another repeat purchase.

　　使用网站上购买的历史数据或浏览记录的数据，企业家可以在营销活动中设计具体的内容和产品推荐。他们可以测试激励（折扣，促销）和其他非激励因素（营销材料的内容），以创造商机吸引重复客户。电子商务公司经常展开限时促销活动。客户必须快速完成购买才能获得特价优惠。此外，您可以自动将优惠券，优惠券添加到购物者的购物车，并在结账过程显示优惠券。此促销活动一举两得：限时交易提高了近期的转换率，优惠券将客户带回网站再次重复消费。

A VIP program takes loyalty points to the next level by giving customers both elevated status and exclusive offers. They enjoy more rewards as they shop. With the reward program, customers purchase repeatedly from the same seller to get more benefits on the money they spent. Align expectations with your customers regularly. Keep in mind that be transparent and honest about what you inform the existing customers. Over-promising and under-delivering is the easiest way to lose trustworthiness. Gaining customer trust goes a long way towards getting consumers to like your brand — so keep everything from product descriptions to promotional activities as accurate as possible similar to the feature and quality of the actual products or services.

VIP计划通过为客户提供高消费级别和独家优惠，将积分计划提升到更高的水平。他们购物时享受更多奖励。通过奖励计划，客户更积极从同一个卖家反复购买，以获得更多的利益。定期与客户保持透明和诚恳的联系。获得客户信任让他们喜欢您的品牌大有帮助 。因此，确保展示产品到促销活动的所有内容，是与实际产品或服务的功能和质量是相同的。

Increasing the transaction value 增加交易价值

　　Increasing the transaction value means you're trying to entice each customer to purchase more in a transaction. It typically does this through a process called upselling or cross-selling. Cross-selling is a selling technique that recommends complementary products that satisfy the unfulfilled needs of the main item. For example, a mouse could be cross-sold to a customer purchasing a personal computer. Often, cross-selling offers consumers the products they would have bought to generate sales at the right time.

　　增加交易价值意味着企业设法让每个客户在交易中购买更多。它通常通过称为追加销售或交叉销售来实现。交叉销售是一种销售技术，推荐满足主要产品未满足需求的补充产品。例如，鼠标可以交叉销售给购买个人计算机的顾客。交叉销售通常为消费者及时提供了他们想购买的产品。

Cross-selling is common to every type of business. For instance, banks and insurance agencies often use cross-selling to increase the value of transaction. Debit cards, credit cards, investment funds, and other financial products are cross-sold to depositors opening a savings account. Insurance agencies suggest life insurance to customers buying a medical card, saving plan. By showing the breadth of a catalog to customers, they are likely to purchase more than intended. E-Commerce website uses the cross-selling technique in sales campaigns, on product pages, and during the checkout process. It is an effective tactic for generating higher sales from a single transaction. Sellers can cross-selling with the product catalogs, and diversifying the existing product range. This will be further earning consumer's confidence to label the seller as the complete solution provider for the type of products.

交叉销售适用于任何业务。例如，银行和保险机构经常使用交叉销售来增加交易价值。借记卡，信用卡，投资基金和其他金融产品交叉出售给开立储蓄账户的存款人。保险代理机构向购买医疗卡，储蓄计划的顾客提供人寿保险。通过向客户展示商品目录，他们可能会购买超过预的产品。电子商务网站在销售活动，产品页面和结账过程中使用交叉销售技术。这是通过单笔交易产生更高销售额的有效策略。交叉销售可以通过产品目录通知用户，让他们知道卖家所提供的商品，进一步赢得他们的信任，将卖家标记为该产品一站式的提供商。

Other than that, up-selling is another effective way to increase average transaction value. Selling the premium, upgraded products or more quantity of the same products to the customer is a direct way to make more sales. Avoid recommending a product or service that is significantly more expensive than the product being purchased. Thus, you may offer the products based on the customer spending power by using the average transaction value, income level, and education, etc.

除此之外，向上销售是提高平均交易价值的另一种有效方式。向客户出售优质，升级产品或更多数量的相同产品是实现更多销售的直接方式。避免推荐比购买产品贵很多的产品或服务。因此，您可以使用平均交易价值，收入水平和教育等，根据客户消费能力提供产品。

For a business-to-business customer, focus on business size and the number of employees. Never hard sell to customers, focus on their actual needs, and explain how the value-added offer will help them meet those needs. As a rule of thumb, if you cannot justify how the additional purchase will benefit the customer's overall goals, then it's not an upsell even worth considering. Not everyone is a viable customer for an upsell, and you should never, ever hard sell additional products or services to a customer who doesn't really need them. For example, if you're considering pitching the premium enterprise resource planning software to a small business owner, but doesn't fit directly into his long-term plan, you shouldn't force it. If you try to sell the product that cannot deliver any positive result to the customer, you not only losing the trust of the customer and potential risk of losing his business altogether.

对于企业对企业客户，请关注业务规模和员工数量。永远不要向客户盲目地销售，专注于他们的实际需求，并解释增值服务如何帮助他们满足这些需求。如果企业无法解释额外购买将如何有利于客户，那么这不是一个值得考虑的追加销售。并非每个客户都是可行的追加销售客户，永远不应该向没有实际需求的客户销售额外的产品或服务。例如，如果您正在考虑将企业资源规划软件投放给小型企业所有者，但不能直接适用于小型企业的长期计划，则不应强迫销售。如果您的产品无法为客户提供任何利益或积极结果，您不仅会失去客户的信任，也能完全失去原有销售的潜在风险。

When meeting with customers, focus on their most concern issues, offer a solution and upsell to them, so business misses no opportunity to create sales. Always promote an upgrade within the context of an idea related to customers' needs. If you see an opportunity to help a customer increases the leads from social platform marketing, come up with a solid plan to help him achieve it. Don't just promote the products for the sake of getting your sales–provide an actionable plan to generate quality leads on the social platform for the customer. Commit to bringing real values to the customers right from day one — and that the products or services can live up with the expectation to deliver the tangible results.

在与客户会面时，关注他们的问题，为他们提供解决方案和追加销售，让企业掌握创造销售的机会。在与客户需求相关的创意背景下促进升级。如果您看到有机会帮助客户增加社交平台营销的潜在客户，请提出一个可靠的计划来帮助他实现这一目标。不要仅仅为了获得销售而推销产品 - 提供可行的计划，以便在客户的社交平台上产生优质的潜在客户。承诺从第一天起就为客户带来真正的价值 - 并且提供可以满足实际需求和提供切实的效果的产品或服务。

Compare side-by-side the features of your products so that the customer can see the benefit of the premium version. When you're proposing an upsell, it's especially important to provide transparent pricing information. Give your customers a complete pricing breakdown and explain the benefit and cost involved. If a customer understands the value of money spent, they'll feel more confident about investing the money on it. Offer the discounted price, bundle in quantities, purchase with purchase, or personalized discount to encourage the customer to make an immediate purchase decision. Successful in-person upselling might require training for the techniques. Understanding how to upsell effectively can generate additional income, but doing it the wrong could turn away existing business.

并排比较产品的功能，以便客户可以看到高级版本的好处。当您提出加售时，提供透明的定价信息尤为重要。为您的客户提供完整的定价细分，并解释所涉及的收益和成本。如果客户理解消费的价值，他们会对投入资金更有信心。提供折扣价，数量捆绑，购买再购买或个性化折扣，以鼓励客户立即做出购买决定。成功的面对面追加销售技巧需要进行培训。了解如何有效地追加销售可以产生额外的收入，但做错了可能会导致现有业务的下滑。

Optimizing prices 优化价格

Optimizing prices mean you'll gain more money from every transaction of your business. A positive relationship does not exist between a company's total revenue and the prices of its products or services. Higher prices do not always lead to better sales for a business. When prices change, a business owner must consider elasticity to gauge the actual impact on the total revenues. Therefore, a change in price can either be positive or negative to the sales.

优化价格意味着您可以从每笔交易中获得更多收益。公司的总收入与其产品或服务的价格之间没有一定的关系。较高的价格并不总能带来更好的销售。当价格发生变化时，企业主必须考虑价格弹性来衡量对总收入的实际影响。因此，价格的变化可能对销售产生正面或负面影响。

The elasticity of demand means the interaction between the demand of the products and its price. When a company raises its prices, the demand from the customers may change in response with a higher price. Therefore, the change in total revenues must consider from both price and demand. A hike in price does not guarantee to result in an increased sale. However, when a company plans to reduce prices, the company must gain additional sales, particularly if the decrease in price is substantial enough to gain huge market share. Here, the surge in the customers' demand may offset the immediate decrease in an average transaction resulting from the cheaper prices.

　　需求弹性意味着产品需求与价格之间的相互作用。当公司提高价格时，客户的需求可能会随着价格的上涨而变化。因此，总收入的变化必须从价格和需求两方面考虑。价格上涨并不能保证增加销售。然而，当一家公司计划降低价格时，公司必须获得额外的销售额，特别是如果价格下降幅度足以获得巨大的市场份额。客户需求的激增可能抵消由于价格较低而导致的平均交易的减少。

To forecast the effect of prices will have on revenue, a company must conduct a research to gauge its impact. By determining the customer's willingness to pay at the micro-level (based on individual data), a company can predict more accurately the actual impact of the price change on the total sales. The main priority when forecasting the net effect of price changes on revenues is the elasticity of demand. For the inelastic market, the customer is price insensitive as the demand does not change with price. In simpler words, the customer will buy the same quantity regardless of price. In an elastic market, the customer is price sensitive since the changes in price results in the significant drop in demand. Therefore, the price surge in the inelastic condition would lead to increased sales. However, a price hike in the elastic market would lead to decreased revenues.

为了预测价格对收入的影响，公司必须进行研究以评估其影响。通过确定客户在微观层面上支付的意愿（基于个人数据），公司可以更准确地预测价格变化对总销售额的实际影响。预测价格变化对收入的净影响时的主要优先事项是了解需求弹性。对于非弹性市场，客户对价格不敏感，因为需求不随价格而变化。简而言之，无论价格如何，客户都会购买相同的数量。在弹性市场中，客户对价格敏感，因为价格的变化导致需求的显着下降。因此，非弹性条件下的价格飙升将导致销售额增加。然而，弹性市场的价格上涨将导致收入减少。

Chapter 7- Cost 第 7 章 - 成本
Financial Cost 财务成本

Cost is the money needed in a process of generating sales via product/service. An entrepreneur needs to understand the various expenses incurred in the business. Cost structures differ from one company to another. Therefore, the expense accounts appearing on a financial statement depend on the cost objects, such as a product, service, project, customer, or business activity. Even within a company, cost structure may vary between product lines, divisions or business units, due to the business activity, it performs.

成本是通过产品/服务产生销售所需的资金。企业家需要了解业务中产生的各种费用。成本结构因公司而异。因此，出现在财务报表中的费用帐户取决于成本项目，例如产品，服务，项目，客户或业务活动。即使在公司内部，由于业务活动，成本结构也可能因产品线，部门或业务部门而异。

Financial costs are expenses that a company incurs via its operations. For instance, the cost of raw materials, semi-finished products, and finished goods along with administrative expenses, such as rent, salaries, insurance, and utilities. Organization record accounting costs in the statement of profit and loss (P/L).

财务成本是公司通过其运营产生的费用。例如，原材料，半成品和成品的成本以及管理费用，如租金，工资，保险和公用事业费。企业将会计成本记录在损益表中的（P／L）。

Operating expenses (OPEX)营业费用（OPEX）

Operating expenses are the costs for a company to run its business operations. Examples include rent, utilities, salaries, costs on sales, general, & administrative (SG&A), research & development, tax; etc. Operational expenses take up the large portion of a company's costs. Entrepreneurs actively look for the measure to reduce operating expenses without causing a significant drop in quality or production of output. In contrast to capital expenditures, operating costs are tax-deductible in the year incurred.

营业费用是公司经营业务的成本。例子包括租金，公用事业，工资，销售成本，一般和行政（SG&A），研发，税收；运营支出占公司成本的很大一部分。企业家积极寻求降低运营成本的措施，确保不会导致质量或产量的显着下降。与资本支出相比，运营成本记录在当下的财政年度并可以抵税。

Capital Expenditures (CAPEX) 资本支出（CAPEX）

Capital expenditures are the costs that companies purchase fixed assets for utilizing for more than a year. For example, a company might have capital expenditures on the assets to get more sales. Fixed assets categorized as non-current assets (building, machine, equipment, vehicles, etc.) from an accounting standpoint as they are not likely to convert into cash in the first year. It normally charges to expense throughout the functional life of the asset, using depreciation.

资本支出是指公司购买固定资产超过一年的成本。例如，公司可能会对资产进行资本支出以获得更多销售额。从会计角度分类为非流动资产（建筑物，机器，设备，车辆等）的固定资产，因为它们在第一年不太可能转换为现金。它通常使用折旧在资产的整个使用寿命期间报销费用。

Capital expenditures might include big-ticket items such as the machine, equipment, vehicle, building (retail store, factory, office), building renovation (expansion, upgrade), hardware (computers, furniture). The industry that a company ventured in largely determines the nature of its capital expenditures. A business should at least maintain the previous level of capital expenditures. Otherwise, it will lead to a decline in business if the reinvestment is inadequate in the organization. A business should increase capital expenditure to ramp-up production if the management foresees the expansion of the business.

资本支出可能包括机器，设备，车辆，建筑物（零售店，工厂，办公室），建筑物翻新（扩建，升级），硬件（计算机，家具）等资产。企业涉及的行业在很大程度上决定了其资本支出的性质。企业至少应保持以前的资本支出水平。否则，如果企业的再投资不足，将导致业务下降。如果管理层预见到业务扩张，企业应增加资本支出以提高产量。

Economic Cost 经济成本

　　Variable cost and fixed cost are the two main costs in the economy. A company's total cost is the sum of the fixed costs and variable costs. Variable costs fluctuate with the output produced. Fixed costs stay the same, no matter how much output produced.

　　可变成本和固定成本是经济成本中的两个主要成本。公司的总成本是固定成本和可变成本的总和。可变成本随产生的产量而波动。无论产量多少，固定成本都保持不变。

Fixed Costs 固定成本

Fixed costs incurred on the regular interval as long as the business thrives. It is most likely maintaining at the same rate in the stipulated period. Examples of fixed costs are overhead costs such as monthly rentals, interest expenses, taxes, amortization, depreciation of fixed assets.

只要业务持续发展，固定成本必然会在定期内产生的。它在规定的时间内保持相同的费用。固定成本的例子如月租金，利息费用，税项，摊销，固定资产折旧。

Certain types of businesses have been high fixed costs, because of the leasing cost on equipment or commercial space. For example, a printing service has substantial costs on the printer, rental of space regardless the volume of business has. However, once those fixed costs reach the breakeven point, it is fairly easy to generate profits from then on due to low variable costs.

由于设备或商业空间的租赁成本，造成某些类型的企业的固定成本很高。例如，无论业务的好坏，打印服务在打印机和商业空间上占据了相当大的成本。然而，一旦这些固定成本达到盈亏平衡点（BEP）后，若可变成本是相对低的，企业就很容易产生利润。

Variable Costs 可变成本

　　Variable costs are expenses that change with the volume of production. Examples of variable costs are the cost that involves directly in the production of goods & services. For instance, direct material cost, labor costs, bonuses, commissions, utilities, and marketing expenses.

　　可变成本是随着生产量而变化的费用。可变成本的例子是直接涉及商品和服务所产生的成本。例如，直接材料成本，人工成本，奖金，佣金，公用事业和营销费用。

A company that aims to increase its profit by cutting costs may need to focus on variable costs for raw materials, direct labor, and advertising. However, the cost-cutting initiatives must be optimized, so it doesn't affect product or service quality, as this would have a negative impact on sales. By reducing the variable costs, a business increases its gross profit margin and eventually leads to a profit-making position easily.

通过削减成本来增加利润的公司可能需要关注原材料，直接人工和广告的可变成本。企业必须优化成本削减计划，才不会影响产品或服务质量，因为这会对销售产生负面影响。通过降低可变成本，企业可以提高其毛利率，并最终轻松获得盈利。

Sunk Cost 沉没成本

Sunk cost is also known as embedded cost, past cost, prior year cost, stranded cost, sunk capital, or retrospective cost. A sunk cost is a cost that has already incurred and cannot be recovered. Thus, Sunk costs are an independent event and should not consider when making future investment or project. To make an informed decision, the business owners only considers the costs and revenues that will fluctuate because of the decision; they do not consider sunk costs. For example, A manufacturing firm may have several sunk costs, such as the cost of equipment, heavy machinery, and the lease cost of a factory. It should exclude these costs when making future investment or project. All sunk costs are fixed costs. However, not all fixed-costs are sunk costs.

沉没成本是已经产生且无法回收的成本。因此，沉没成本是一项独立事件，在进行未来投资或项目时不应将其纳入考量。为做出明智的决定，企业只考虑决策而产生波动的成本和收入；而不考虑沉没成本。例如，制造商可能有几个沉没成本，例如设备成本，重型机械和工厂的租赁成本。在进行未来的投资或项目时，应排除这些成本。所有沉没成本都是固定成本。但是，并非所有固定成本都是沉没成本。

Opportunity Cost 机会成本

Opportunity cost represents the benefits business misses out on when choosing one option over another. While financial reports do not show opportunity cost, entrepreneurs can use it to make informed decisions when they have multiple choices in hands.

机会成本代表了企业在选择一种选择时错失的的机会代价。虽然财务报告没有显示机会成本，但企业家可以在多种选择时使用它来做出明智的决策。

When assessing the profitability of investments or projects, businesses pick for the best option that is likely to generate the greatest return from all available options. However, businesses must also consider the opportunity cost of other available alternatives. Assume that, given a capital for investment, a business must choose between investing funds in a new business or using it to purchase new machinery. No matter which option the business chooses, the potential profit it gives up on the abandon option is the opportunity cost.

在评估投资或项目的盈利能力时，企业会选择从所有可用选项中获得最大回报的最佳选择。但是，企业还必须考虑其他可用替代选择的机会成本。假设有一笔投资资金，企业必须选择在新业务中投资或使用它来购买新机器。无论选择哪种方案，放弃的潜在利益都是机会成本。

The formula for Calculating Opportunity Cost 计算机会成本的公式

Opportunity cost is the difference between the expected returns of each option: Opportunity cost = return of abandon option - the return of the chosen option. For example, an entrepreneur has two investment opportunities.
Option 1 Invest in the stock market with 0%-10% return, since the value of an investment depends on its market value.
Option 2 Reinvest in newer equipment with 8% return. It will enhance the operating efficiency and revenues.

机会成本是每个选项的预期收益之间的差异：机会成本=放弃选项的回报 - 选项的回报。例如，企业家有两个投资机会。

选项1投资于股票市场，回报率为0%-10%，因为投资价值取决于其市场价值。

选项2重新投资新设备，回报率为8%。它将提高运营效率和收入。

	Oppurtunity cost =	Option not chosen Equipment	Option chosen Stock Market
WORST CASE	8.0%	8%	0%
	7.0%	8%	1%
	6.0%	8%	2%
	5.0%	8%	3%
	4.0%	8%	4%
	3.0%	8%	5%
	2.0%	8%	6%
	1.0%	8%	7%
	0.0%	8%	8%
	-1.0%	8%	9%
BEST CASE	-2.0%	8%	10%

Scenario 1

Risk-taking business owner chooses investment in stock market.

The worst case is 8% of opportunity cost when the equity value wipes out completely, with less 8% of the return when investing in equity. The best cast is -2% of opportunity cost when the equity value gains 10%, with an additional 2% to return when investing in equity.

Upside potential is 2%; downside potential is 8%.

	机会成本=	未选择选项 设备	选择选项 股市
最糟糕的案例	8.0%	8%	0%
	7.0%	8%	1%
	6.0%	8%	2%
	5.0%	8%	3%
	4.0%	8%	4%
	3.0%	8%	5%
	2.0%	8%	6%
	1.0%	8%	7%
	0.0%	8%	8%
	-1.0%	8%	9%
最佳的案例	-2.0%	8%	10%

情景 1

冒险的企业家选择在股票市场投资。最糟糕的情况是，当股权价值完全消失时，机会成本为 8%，投资股票时的回报率低于 8% 的设备投资。当股权价值增加 10% 时，最佳投资是机会成本的 -2%，投资股权时还有 2% 的回报。

上行潜力为 2%；下行潜力为 8%。

	Oppurtunity cost =	Option not chosen	Option chosen
		Stock Market	Equipment
BEST CASE	-8.0%	0%	8%
	-7.0%	1%	8%
	-6.0%	2%	8%
	-5.0%	3%	8%
	-4.0%	4%	8%
	-3.0%	5%	8%
	-2.0%	6%	8%
	-1.0%	7%	8%
	0.0%	8%	8%
	1.0%	9%	8%
WORST CASE	2.0%	10%	8%

Scenario 2

Risk-averse business owner chooses the investment on equipment.

The worst case is 2% of opportunity cost when the equity earns the full expected return of 10%, with 2% less of return when investing in equipment.

The best cast -8% of opportunity cost when the equity value wipes out completely, an additional 8% of return when investing in equipment.

Upside potential is 8%, downside potential is 2%.

	机会成本=	未选择选项 股市	选择选项 设备
最糟糕的案例	8.0%	8%	0%
	7.0%	8%	1%
	6.0%	8%	2%
	5.0%	8%	3%
	4.0%	8%	4%
	3.0%	8%	5%
	2.0%	8%	6%
	1.0%	8%	7%
	0.0%	8%	8%
	-1.0%	8%	9%
最佳的案例	-2.0%	8%	10%

情景 2

规避风险的企业主选择对设备的投资。最糟糕的情况是机会成本的 2%，当股权获得 10%的全部预期回报时，投资设备的回报减少 2%。

当股权价值完全消失时，最佳投机机会成本占 8%，投资设备时获得 8%的回报。上行潜力为 8%，下行潜力为 2%。

 It is important to compare investment options with risk consideration. It is a safer choice in scenario 2 since the reward is greater (8%) than risk (2%). On the other hands, scenario 1 is the riskier option since the risk (8%) is higher than reward (2%).

Thus, scenario 2 is a better choice of investment with less opportunity cost and higher return.

将投资选择与风险考虑进行比较非常重要。在情景 2 中，这是一个更安全的选择，因为回报（8%）高过风险（2%）。另一方面，情景 1 是风险较高的选择，因为风险（8%）高于奖励（2%）。因此，方案 2 是更好的投资选择，机会成本更低，回报更高。

Opportunity cost analysis plays an important role in deciding the capital structure of the business. Funding via both equity and debt require an expense. For debt, interest payment is the cost of funding to compensate lenders. For equity, the return or dividends are the cost of funding to compensate the risk shareholders. Each option also bears an opportunity cost. Therefore, entrepreneurs must choose the right mix of capital structure. They need to optimize the capital structure by considering risk and reward of all options to maximize the value of the company.

　　机会成本分析在决定业务的资本结构方面起着重要作用。通过股权和债务融资需要支出。对于债务，利息支付是补偿贷方的资金成本。对于股权而言，回报或股息是补偿股东风险的资金成本。每个选项也有机会成本。因此，企业家必须选择合适的资本结构组合。他们需要通过考虑所有期权的风险和回报来优化资本结构，以最大化公司的价值。

Economies of Scale 规模经济

　　The economy of scale is the cost-benefit that a company gains with an increased quantity of a specific good or service. The quantity of output and the fixed costs are in an inverse relationship. Put simply, as the number of goods and services increase, marginal cost will drop.

规模经济是公司通过增加特定商品或服务的数量而获得的成本效益。产出数量和固定成本呈反比关系。简而言之，随着商品和服务数量的增加，边际成本将下降。

For example, consider a cup maker. Each cup produced requires $0.50 of porcelain. The factory incurs $200 dollars of fixed costs every month. If the factory makes 100 cups, then each cup incurs $2.00 ($200/100unit) of fixed costs. Therefore, the total cost per cup, including the porcelain, would be $2.50 ($2.50= $0.50+ ($200/100units)).

例如，考虑一个杯子制造商。每个生产的杯子需要 0.50 元的瓷器。该工厂每个月产生 200 元的固定成本。如果工厂生产 100 杯，则每杯产生 2.00 元（200元/ 100 单位）的固定成本。因此，每杯

（包括瓷器）的总成本为2.50元（2.50元= 0.50元+（200元/100单位））。

However, if the factory increased the production unit to 200 cups per month, then each cup would cost only $1.00 ($200/200units) of fixed cost. This happens because the fixed-costs shared between more units of output. The total cost per cup would then drop to $1.50 ($1.50 = $0.50+ ($200/200units)). Therefore, marginal cost reduces $1.00 when the 100 unit increases to 200 units of production. In this situation, increasing production volume causes the total cost decreases significantly.

但是，如果工厂将生产单位增加到每月200杯，则每个杯子的固定成本仅为1.00元（200元/ 200单位）。这是因为固定成本在更多单位产出之间共享。每杯的总成本将降至1.50元（1.50元= 0.50元+（200元/ 200单位））。因此，当100个单位增加到200个单位时，边际成本会减少1.00美元。在这种情况下，增加产量会导致总成本显着下降。

When the fixed costs covered, the marginal cost per unit goes down. At lower marginal costs, additional units represent increasing profit margins. It gives price competitiveness for a seller offers an item in bulk. Warehouse retailers (Walmart, Costco, Tesco) leverage on the economy of scale by buying in bulk and packaging in a smaller unit for sale.

当固定成本覆盖后，每单位的边际成本下降。在较低的边际成本下，额外的单位代表着不断增加的利润率。它为卖家提供价格竞争力来提供批量商品。仓库零售商（沃尔玛，好市多，乐购）通过批量购买和小型包装出售来实现规模经济。

Although an economy of scale may seem beneficial to a company, it has limitations. Marginal costs never decrease indefinitely. At some point, operations become too big to keep experiencing economies of scale. This typically follows the law of diminishing returns where a further increase in output will cause an even greater increase in average total cost. This is the concept of diseconomies of scale. It forces companies to innovate business ideas, improve working capital or optimizing the level of production to remain competitive.

  虽然规模经济似乎对公司有利，但它有局限性。边际成本永远不会无限减少。在某些时候，运营变得太大，无法继续经历规模经济。这通常遵循收益递减规律，产量的进一步增加将导致平均总成本的更大幅度增加。这是规模不经济的概念。它迫使公司创新经营理念，改善营运资金或优化生产水平以保持竞争力。

Economies of Scope 范围经济

The economy of scope means the average total cost of a company's production decreases when there is a variation of goods made. The economy of scope provides the cost benefit to a company. This happens when it made a range of products while focusing on its related business's core competencies. One easy way to think about the economy of scope is to imagine that it's cheaper to manufacture two products by sharing the same resources.

范围经济意味着当产品变化时，公司生产的平均总成本会降低。范围经济为公司提供成本效益。这种情况发生在制造一系列产品的同时关注其相关业务的核心竞争力。理解范围经济的一种简单方法，想象通过共享相同的资源来制造两种产品会更经济实惠。

Economies of scope are important for the company, especially for a large corporation, and it can go about achieving the aim in three main ways. The economies of scope can be attained by improving internal efficiency via related diversification. For instance, Procter and Gamble manufacture the range of hygienic products under the different brand name using existing production line and business support unit.

范围经济对公司来说很重要，特别是对于大公司而言，它可以通过三种主要方式实现目标。通过相关的多样化提高内部效率以实现范围经济。例如，宝洁公司使用现有的生产线和业务支持部门，以不同的品牌名称生产各种卫生产品。

Merger and acquisition deals are another way to achieve economies of scope. Two companies with a similar line of business may merge with each other to produce goods or services using the same resources. It makes the simultaneous manufacturing of different products more cost-effective than manufacturing them on their own. For example, Google acquired Android, with joint efforts. They launch the Android operating system for handheld devices successfully within a few years with only a fraction of cost. Today, Android has become the duopoly player of the mobile OS in par with Apple OS, defeating competitors like BlackBerry, Symbian, BlackBerry, and even Windows phone platform.

并购交易是实现范围经济的另一种方式。具有相似业务线的两家公司可以相互合并，使用相同的资源生产商品或服务。它使得不同产品的同时制造比单独制造它们更具成本效益。例如，Google 通过共同努力收购了 Android。他们在几年内成功推出了适用于手持设备的 Android 操作系统，成本仅为其一小部分。今天，Android 已经成为移动操作系统的双寡头，与 Apple OS 相提并论，击败了黑莓，Symbian，甚至 Windows 手机平台等竞争对手。

    Finally, a company may achieve economies of scope via vertical integration by the joint utilization of inputs and leads to reductions in unit costs. Two ways of integration: backward integration and forward integration. A company acquires the supply chain is practicing backward integration. A company that expands toward the front into distribution and point of sale is practicing forward integration. Apple Inc. is one of the best-known companies for vertical integration. Apple manufactures its custom A-series chips, touch ID fingerprint sensor, LCD and OLED screen using its own manufacturing plant. The Apple premium reseller model, where the company's products sell at the company-licensed distributor, this allows the business to control the distribution of the product to the end user.

COMPARISON	ECONOMIES OF SCALE	ECONOMIES OF SCOPE
Meaning	Economies of scale gains cost advantage due to the increasing number of output produced, using common resources	Economies of scope refers to savings in cost due to the production of multiple products, using common resources
Resources	Large quantities of similar raw materials using common resources	Varieties of raw materials using common resources
Task Complexity	Relatively simple planning	More complex scheduling and planning
Cost Reduction	Average total cost of one product	Average total cost of multiple products
Cost Advantage	Due to volume	Due to variation
Production	Fixed production line	Flexible production line
Product line	Standardization of product	Diversification product

最后，公司可以通过联合利用资源来垂直整合实现范围经济，从而降低单位成本。两种集成方式：后向集成和前向集成。一家公司收购供应链实行向后整合。向前发展为分销和销售点扩展的公司实施前向整合。 Apple Inc.是垂直整合领域最知名的公司之一。 Apple 使用自己的制造工厂生产定制 A 系列芯片，触摸式 ID 指纹传感器，LCD 和 OLED 屏幕。Apple 高级经销商，公司的产品在公司许可的分销商处销售，这使得企业可以控制产品向最终用户的分销。

对比	经济规模	范围经济
含义	由于使用共同资源产生的产量增加，规模经济获得了成本优势	范围经济是指使用共同资源生产多种产品所节省的成本
资源	使用共同资源的大量类似原材料	使用共同资源的各种原材料
任务复杂性	规划比较简单	更复杂的调度和计划
降低成本	一种产品的平均总成本	多种产品的平均总成本
成本优势	数量	多元化
生产	固定生产线	灵活的生产线
生产线	产品标准化	多元化产品

Cost Control & Performance Management
成本控制与绩效管理

Cost control by the management means a search for better and more economical ways of performing an activity in an organization. Cost control is the prevention of waste of resources within the organization. It is the practice of identifying and reducing business expenses to increase profits. It is also an important factor for maintaining and growing profitability. Businesses use outsourcing to control costs because many businesses find it cheaper to pay a third party to perform certain non-core or peripheral tasks rather than accomplish everything on their own. Cost controls rely on the past trend to make an informed decision on the present situation. Cost control applies to procedures, processes or activities, which have common standards. It seeks to attain the lowest cost optimizing the use of resources.

  成本控制意味着企业在寻求更好和更经济的方法执行商业活动。成本控制是防止组织内的资源浪费。这是减少业务费用以增加利润的做法。这也是维持和提高盈利能力的重要因素。企业使用外包来控制成本，因为许多企业发现支付第三方执行某些非核心或外围任务会比自己完成所有任务会更便宜。成本控制需分析过去的趋势，对目前的情况作出明智的决定。成本控制适用于具有共同标准的程序，过程或活动。它力求以最低的成本优化资源的使用。

Entrepreneurs need to review both fixed and variable costs and try to reduce the expenses. Latter costs should be the focus since it changes with the volume of sales. The cost of goods sold (COGS) is a variable cost that can optimize significantly. It can be optimized by searching for suppliers to source items at more competitive prices. Bargaining with an existing supplier to get better deals in terms of lower unit cost, quantity discount, payment terms are among the ways to reduce COGS. It is difficult to reduce fixed costs, such as the salary, lease payment, utility because they usually fix in the stipulated period to sustain the business operation.

企业家需要审查固定成本和可变成本，并尝试减少开支。可变成本应该成为焦点，因为它会随着销售量的增加而变化。销售成本（COGS）是可变成本，可以显着优化。可以通过搜索供应商以更具竞争力的价格来源项目来优化它。与现有供应商讨价还价以获得更低的单位成本，数量折扣，付款条件等更优惠的交易是降低COGS的方法之一。企业很难降低固定成本，例如工资，租赁付款，公用事业，因为这些费用需要在规定的时间内支付以维持业务运营。

Budgetary control 预算控制

A budget is the prospect of financial statements such as P&L, cash flow, balance sheet. Budgeting refers to the formulation of the plan in numerical terms for a financial year. Budgetary cost control is the control activity that uses the budget to control cost. A variance is defined as the difference between budgeted amount and actual results. Entrepreneurs use the variance to identify critical areas that need a change. They must emphasize the largest dollar variance on company results. If the actual cost is more than the budget, they can exercise the control measure to reduce the cost to the budgeted amount or amend with a new reasonable budget plan. On the other hands, if expenses less than the budget without compromising the quality of the output, they must implement good practice within the organization. Some businesses analyze percentage variances and take-action on those actual costs that have the largest percentage variance from the budgeted costs.

　　预算是财务报表的如损益表，现金流量，资产负债表的预测。预算编制是指在一个财政年度以数字形式制定计划。预算成本控制是使用预算来控制成本和商业活动。方差定义为预算金额与实际结果之间的差异。企业家使用方差来识别需要改变的关键项目。他们必须关注公司费用的最大价值差异。企业也可以分析了与预算成本差异最大的实际成本的百分比差异来采取必要的策列。如果实际成本高于预算,他们可以采取控制措施,将成本降低到预算金额,或者用新的合理预算计划进行修改。另一方面,如果费用低于预算而不影响产出质量,企业必须在组织内实施这些良好做法。

Horizontal analysis 水平分析

  Horizontal analysis or trend analysis is a financial statement analysis technique that shows differences in the financial statement items with at least two periods of comparison. It is an effective tool to examine the trend. Typically, the comparison is made between two or more periods. The analysis is conducted by comparing the absolute monetary value items in the financial statements. For example, Entrepreneurs can compare cash in hand in the current to other accounting periods. Another method is via the percentage variance using the earliest period as the base period to compare with a later period on the item of the financial statements. The changes can be shown both in dollars and percentage. They can conduct the horizontal analysis for cash flow, income statement, balance sheet. This method is helpful in identifying the items which are changing the most. The difference of amount and percentage term computed by using the following formulas:

  水平分析或趋势分析是一种财务报表分析技术，它显示财务报表项目与至少两个比较期间的差异。它是检查趋势的有效工具。通常，在两个或更多个时段之间进行比较。通过比较财务报表中项目的货价值进行分析。例如，企业家可以将当前的现金与其他时段进行比较。另一种方法是通过使用早期的的财务报表项目百分比差异作为基准期来与后期进行比较。这些变化可以以货币价值和百分比显示。水平分析可以对现金流量，损益表，资产负债表进行横向分析。此方法有助于识别变化最大的项目。使用以下公式计算的金额和百分比项的差异：

Amount Difference:
The variance of an amount: Value of current period-Value of the base period

Percentage variance: （Variance of amount/ Value of base period ）X 100

金额差异：
金额的方差：当期的价值 - 基期的价值

百分比方差：（金额的方差/基期的价值）X 100

  The horizontal analysis allows a company owner to see what has been driving a company's financial performance. It helps to spot the seasonal trend over the period of comparison. It enables the business owner to assess relative changes in different line items over the period of comparison. By looking at the income statement, entrepreneurs can examine the revenue and costs on what has been driving a company's financial performance, particularly profitability.

For cash flow trend analysis, the healthy cash flow trend shows a business is in a stable position to fulfill the business obligations. While a business can borrow money to get through the shortfall of cash to prevent defaults or foreclosures. Cash flow differs from the actual cash position. Having cash is important while positive cash flow shows the capability to generate and use cash.

横向分析允许公司所有者了解推动公司业绩的因素。它有助于发现比较期间的季节性趋势。它使企业家能够评估比较期间不同行项目的相对变化。通过查看损益表，企业家可以检查推动公司财务业绩的收入和成本，尤其是盈利能力。对于现金流量趋势分析，健康的现金流趋势表明企业处于履行业务义务(摊还债务)的稳定位置。虽然企业可以借钱来弥补现金短缺，以防止违约或取消抵押品赎回权。现金流量与实际现金有所不同。拥有现金非常重要，而正现金流则显示了生成和使用现金的能力。

Horizontal analysis can be linked to the key performance index (KPI) such as inventory turnover, profit margin. It can detect emerging issues and strengths of the business. For example, net profit may have been surging because the falling cost of goods sold, or because of the growing revenues. Other KPI, like the cash flow-to-debt ratio and the interest coverage ratio, shows the ability of a company to service its debt with cash. Horizontal analysis is also an easier approach to compare growth rates and profitability between different companies.

横向分析可以与关键绩效指标（KPI）互相关联，例如库存周转率，利润率。它可以检测出业务出现的问题或优势。例如，由于销售成本下降或收入增加，净利润可能一直在飙升。其他关键绩效指标，如现金流量与债务比率和利息覆盖率，显示了公司用现金偿还债务的能力。横向分析也是比较不同公司之间增长率和盈利能力的更简单方法。

Vertical analysis 垂直分析

  Vertical analysis is the proportional analysis of a financial statement. This analysis converted each item on a financial statement into a percentage of the base item. This means that all items on an income statement converted into a percentage of gross sales, while every item on a balance sheet calculated as a percentage of total assets.

垂直分析分析是财务报表的比例分析。此分析将财务报表中的每个项目转换为基本项目的百分比。这意味着损益表中的所有项目都转换为总销售额的百分比，而资产负债表上的每个项目都计算为总资产的百分比。

The most common application of vertical analysis is within a financial statement for a single time period. It enables entrepreneurs to see the relative proportion's comparison with the percentage (as the similar benchmark). In an income statement, every item is stated as a percentage of gross sales. It is also suitable for timeline analysis, to observe the difference in accounts, for two- or more-year comparison. For example, if the cost of goods sold has a history of being 40% of sales in the past two years, then a new percentage of 48% of the most recent year shows the significant rise of cost, the business owner may need to reexamine the efficiency of the procurement process, or seeks the alternative suppliers for better deals.

　　垂直分析的最常见应用是在一个时段的财务报表中。它使企业家能够看到相对比例与百分比的比较（以类似的基准）。在损益表中，每个项目都表示为总销售额的百分比。它也适用于不同时段分析，以两年或更多年的比较来观察账户差异。例如，如果销售商品的成本在过去两年占有40%的销售，那么最近一年48%的百分比显示成本显着上升，企业家可能需要重新审查采购流程的效率，或寻求替代供应商以获得更好的交易。

For the balance sheet, every item is converted as a percentage of total assets. This analysis can examine the capital structure. It shows the right mix of equity and debt in comparison with total assets. For an example, if the total asset is $1000,000, account payable is $100,000 or

10% of the total assets. The account receivable is $ 150,000 or 15% of total assets. The current assets (account receivable) are higher than current liabilities (account payable). Therefore, the working capital is sufficient to meet the short-term obligations.

对于资产负债表，每个项目都将转换为总资产的百分比。这种分析可以检验资本结构。它显示了与总资产相比的权益和债务的组合。例如，如果总资产为 1000,000 元，则应付账款为 100,000 元或总资产的 10%。应收账款为 150,000 元，占总资产的 15%。流动资产（应收账款）高于流动负债（应付账款）。因此，营运资金足以应付短期债务。

Entrepreneurs can compare the percentage with previous year figure. They can observe the trends and have a better understanding of the financial position of their company. If the equity is shrinking, while the asset is rising. It indicated the invested asset may not be effective in generating enough revenues, creating value for shareholders. Entrepreneurs must develop new strategies to change operation activity using the asset efficiently. Such period to period comparisons enabled entrepreneurs to identify issues and underlying causes of it. They may take the right action to solve the problem instantly.

　　企业家可以将百分比与上一年的数字进行比较。他们可以观察趋势并更好地了解公司的财务状况。如果股权正在萎缩，那么资产正在飙升。它表明，过度投资资产可能无法有效创造更多的收入，为股东创造价值。企业家必须制定新战略，以有效地利用资产来改变经营活动增加收入。垂直分析使企业家能够识别问题的根源。他们可以采取应对措施立即解决问题。

www.ingramcontent.com/pod-product-compliance
Lightning Source LLC
Chambersburg PA
CBHW030613220526
45463CB00004B/1285